P9-DBJ-199

BENJAMIN HARRISON
1833-1901

Chronology-Documents-Bibliographical Aids

Edited by
HARRY J. SIEVERS, S.J.
Professor of History
Fordham University

Series Editor
HOWARD F. BREMER

1969
OCEANA PUBLICATIONS, INC.
Dobbs Ferry, New York

© Copyright Oceana Publications, Inc. 1969
Library of Congress Catalog Card Number 74-83746
Oceana Book No. 303-9

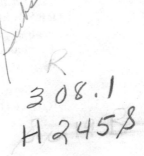

308.1
H245b

Printed in the United States of America

92686°

CONTENTS

BIBLIOGRAPHICAL AIDS

EDITOR'S FOREWORD

In this Chronology every attempt has been made to cite the most accurate dates. Diaries, letters, newspapers, official documents, and similar evidence have been used to determine the exact date. In the few instances where there has been conflicting evidence, the more plausible date has been chosen.

This is a research tool compiled primarily for the student. Obviously the selection of significant events and of key documents implies a subjective judgment. It is hoped, however, that this judgment is reasoned because it is based on a long acquaintance with the Benjamin Harrison Papers and with his role in American History.

The purpose of this book is to make available some pertinent facts and key documents **plus** a critical bibliography that might stimulate the student to investigate for himself additional and/or contradictory material. The works cited may not always be available in small libraries, yet a majority of titles can now be had in paperback editions. Documents in this volume are taken from Benjamin Harrison, **Public Papers and Addresses Of,** Charles Hedges (Compiler), **Speeches of Benjamin Harrison, Twenty-third President of the United States,** Mary Lord Harrison (Compiler), **Views of An Ex-President,** Harry J. Sievers, **Benjamin Harrison** (3 vols.), and Henry Steele Commager, **Documents in American History.** Students are also referred to James D. Richardson, **Messages and Papers of the Presidents** in which the volume on Harrison will be available in most reference libraries.

CHRONOLOGY

YOUTH

1833

August 20   Born: North Bend, Ohio. Father: John Scott Harrison. Mother: Elizabeth Ramsey Irwin.

1840

November 3   Grandfather William Henry Harrison elected 9th President of U.S.

1841

March 4   "Old Tippecanoe" Harrison inaugurated; read 8,578 word inaugural, the then longest on record.

April 4   First President to die in White House.

1841-1847

Attended North Bend log cabin school; also tutored at home with brothers and sisters.

1847

November 3   At 14 attended Cary's Academy (later called Farmers' College) Cincinnati, Ohio. Influenced by Dr. Robert Hamilton Bishop, an Edinburgh Scot, known as Father of American Sociology.

1850

August 15   Mother died at 40.

1

September 30   Entered Miami University, the "Yale of the West," at Oxford, Ohio, as a junior. Courted Caroline (Carrie) Scott, daughter of Rev. Dr. John W. Scott.

1851

January (30)   Embraced Presbyterianism; planned to study for ministry; interests turned to law; joined Phi Delta Theta, legal fraternity, as 13th charter member.

1852

June 24   Graduated with A.B. degree (Honors) from Miami at 19. Commencement speech described "Poor of England."

Autumn   Read law in Cincinnati offices of Hon. Bellamy Storer, a former Whig congressman.

1853

October 20   Married Caroline Scott.

November   Father (John Scott Harrison) is elected to House of Representatives, as Whig from Ohio.

1854

April 4   Admitted to Ohio bar; moved to Indianapolis, Indiana; appointed court crier at $2.50 per day. Won early cases; assisted City Attorney.

August 12   Son, Russell, born; named for Carrie's brother-in-law, Russell Farnum Lord.

1855

March   Formed law partnership with William Wallace, son of ex-Governor David Wallace of Indiana; met brother Lew Wallace, later author of *Ben Hur*; appointed Commissioner of the Court of Claims.

1856

June

Broke with political faith of father and grandfather (Whigs) by espousing Republicanism; stumps for presidential candidate John C. Fremont on anti-slavery issue.

1857

May 5

Elected on Republican ticket City Attorney with salary of $400 a year.

1858

January 1

Diary resolution: "Stopped use of tobacco in every form." Soon reverted to cigar smoking.

April 3

"Our Little Girl Born About Noon"—diary record of birth of Mary (Mamie) Harrison.

July 10

Refused to be candidate for state legislature, but accepted secretaryship of GOP State Central Committee.

1859

December

Sought nomination as Supreme Court Reporter for Indiana.

1860

February 22

Won nomination; campaigned on anti-slavery plank: "As long as God allows the vital current to flow through my veins, I will never, never, by word or thought, by mind or will, aid in admitting to one rood of Free Territory the Everlasting Curse of Human Bondage."

October 9

Won Reportership by 9,688 votes. Campaigned for Abraham Lincoln.

1861

February 11

President-elect Lincoln's visit to Indianapolis left lasting impression.

April 12   First volume of Court decisions published on day Fort
                Sumter was fired on.

June   Lost third child, a daughter, at birth.

December 11   Wallace and Harrison law partnership ended; new firm
                formed with William P. Fishback.

CIVIL WAR YEARS

1862

July 1   Lincoln's call for 300,000 more Union volunteers.

July 9   Visited Indiana Governor Oliver Morton to volunteer;
                appointed second lieutenant to organize 70th Regiment of
                Indiana Volunteers.

July 22   Promoted to captaincy.

August 8   Made full colonel.

August 13   Broke training camp at Indianapolis; led troops to Ken-
                tucky front.

September 30-   Scored first victory over Confederates at Russellville, Ken-
October 1   tucky.

November 10   Assigned to Ward's Brigade; joined Dumont's Division
                at Scottsville, Kentucky.

November 24   Ordered to guard Louisville and Nashville Railroad tracks
                between Gallatin and Nashville.

1863

January-   Pursued reserve and scavenger duty in Tennessee as prep-
December   aration for campaign to take Atlanta.

1864

January 2   Ordered to front; commanded Ward's Brigade and joined
                "Fighting Joe" Hooker.

February 23   Renominated in *absentia* for office of Supreme Court Reporter.

March 4-11   Reached soil of Georgia; joined Major General Oliver O. Howard; won title of "Administrative Ben."

May 14-15   At Resaca, Georgia, won "the first battle of magnitude" in the celebrated Georgia Campaign; as commander of Ward's Brigade, is cited for gallantry.

May 26-28   Engagement at New Hope Church, Georgia.

June 15   Battle of Golgotha Church, Georgia.

July 20   Cold steel at Peach Tree Creek, Georgia, won promise of brigadier's star by General Hooker.

September 2   Atlanta falls to Union troops.

September 12   Leaves front for first time in over two years.

September 20   Home on furlough; conferred with Governor O. P. Morton.

September 27- October 11   Campaigned in Indiana; won re-election as Court Reporter by 20,000 votes.

October- November   Made successful canvass for Lincoln's re-election.

November 8   Ordered to Georgia front to join Sherman's march to the sea.

December 15-31   Diverted en route; led temporary brigade during Battle of Nashville.

1865

January 1   Second furlough at Indianapolis.

January 30   Felled by scarlet fever at Honesdale, Pennsylvania.

February 23   Brevetted brigadier general.

March 2	Reached Hilton Head, South Carolina, to drill reinforcements.
April 19	At Raleigh learned of Lincoln's assassination. Eulogized slain President.
April 30-May 20	Marched from Raleigh to Richmond and Washington.
May 24	Grand Review in D.C.
June 8	Discharged from Army at 32.
June 10	Saw father en route to Indianapolis; advised that Congressional medal, awarded to General William Henry Harrison, would be bequeathed to him.

VETERAN TURNED CIVILIAN

July	Joined new firm of Porter, Harrison and Fishback; resumed duties as Court Reporter; refused to run for Congress.
July 25	Arranged for General Sherman's reception.
August	As radical reconstructionist crusaded for Negro suffrage.
September 25	Welcomed General Grant to Indianapolis.

1866-1868

Practiced art of practical politics; during Presidential campaign of 1868 is styled as "one of the ablest speakers in the West."

1869

January 15	Relinquished Reporter's office.
February-March	Won fame as public prosecutor with a conviction in Nancy Clem murder case; spoken of as potential candidate for governor in 1872.

July 20   Began long association with "Boys in Blue."

December 15-16 Joined Society of Army of the Cumberland; hosted Indianapolis reception for General George H. Thomas.

1870

September 13   Took stump for congressional candidate, Lew Wallace, future author of *Ben Hur*. (Wallace lost by 393 out of 30,685 votes.)

September 20   Made vacation trip to Niagara Falls.

November 30   Welcomed Judge Cyrus C. Hines to law partnership to replace Fishback who resigned.

December   Death of brother, Irwin Harrison.

1871

May   Appointed by President Grant to defend U.S. Government in Milligan case.

May 29   Victory in Milligan case resulted in national recognition.

1872

January 1-31   Boomed for governor in a pre-convention campaign.

February 22   Lost nomination to General Tom Browne; declined Congressman-at-large candidacy.

July 3   Refused second time to make congressional race.

July 19   Opened GOP campaign by attacking Horace Greeley and the Liberal Republican movement.

November   Re-election of U.S. Grant.

1873

September   Despite failure by Jay Cooke and Co. and depression, law
                 firm prospered; sent children to boarding schools.

1874

April   William Henry Harrison Miller (future U.S. Attorney
                 General) replaced Albert G. Porter in law firm of Harrison,
                 Hines and Miller.

Fall-Winter   Built new brick home on North Delaware Street property
                 purchased in 1867. Home completed and occupied in 1875;
                 in 1960's declared a national historical landmark with
                 title of Benjamin Harrison Memorial Home.

1875

August 18   Dr. and Mrs. John W. Scott, parents of Mrs. Harrison,
                 celebrated golden wedding anniversary.

September   Won Ida Fawkner case involving reform of city's Deaf
                 and Dumb Institute.

October 14   Founding of Seventieth Indiana Regimental Association;
                 elected first president, and re-elected annually until death
                 in 1901.

December 6   Issued formal letter declining gubernatorial candidacy
                 in 1876.

December 10   Rumored as dark horse "presidential aspirant."

1876

January 26   Won "Whiskey Ring" case in Federal Court but incurred
                 Judge Walter Q. Gresham's lifelong hostility.

February 22   Chosen as presidential elector-at-large.

March 1   Death of mother-in-law, Mrs. John W. Scott.

August 2	GOP gubernatorial candidate, Godlove Orth, withdrew under fire.
August 4	Drafted to make race vs. Democrat "Blue Jeans" Williams.
August 6	Candidacy accepted after pressure by General Garfield of Ohio.
August 18	"Bloody Shirt" and "sound money" campaign opened at Danville.
October 10	Beaten in governorship race by 5,000 in 420,000-vote contest. Led ticket by some 2,000 votes.
October 18-25	Campaigned for Rutherford B. Hayes in Chicago and in Philadelphia; also stumped New Jersey, Illinois and Indiana.
November 11-18	Refused President Grant's request to serve as a "visiting statesman" overseeing electoral counts in Louisiana and South Carolina.

1877

February 24	Considered by President-elect Hayes for Cabinet post.
May 5	Broke politically with Senator O.P. Morton.
June	Son, Russell, graduated from Lafayette College, Easton, Pennsylvania.
July 23-25	During railroad strike headed Committee of Public Safety and mediated a strike settlement.
August 4	Squelched talk of candidacy for U.S. Senate.
November 1	Senator Morton's death; emergence as party leader.
December 1	Death of brother-in-law, Major Henry Scott.

1878

May 26	Sudden death of father, John Scott Harrison.

May 31	"The Harrison Horror". Father's grave robbed by ghouls.
June 5	Addressed GOP State Convention.
June 6	Prosecuted grave robbers in Cincinnati.

1879

January 11	Delivered paper on "The Chinese Question" to Indianapolis Literary Club.
Spring	Gained verdict for U.S. Government in "Election Fraud" cases, defeating Thomas A. Hendricks and David Turpie, counsel for defense.
June 28	Appointed by President Hayes to Mississippi River Commission.
July 22	As charter member of Indiana State Bar Association, represented group at National Bar Association first meeting at Saratoga, New York, in August.
August 4	Visited President Hayes at White House; accepted Mississippi River Commission appointment.
October 3	Return visit by President and Mrs. Hayes to Indianapolis home.

1880

January-February	Boomed as both "dark horse" presidential candidate and as vice presidential mate to Blaine.
March 8	Advised Young Republicans that "party may not always have been right," but "it has always been nearer right than any political party that has existed contemporaneously."
June 2-10	At Chicago, attended longest GOP National Convention on record; favored Blaine for 34 ballots; on 35th ballot, following Wisconsin's break, threw Indiana delegation to James A. Garfield; talked of as potential running mate to Ohioan; seconded Conkling's motion for Garfield's unanimous nomination.

Summer and Fall	Took prominent part in party councils on national as well as state level; campaigned widely.
October 12	Former law partner, Albert G. Porter, elected to governorship of Indiana.
November 4	Election of President Garfield; learned Harrison preferred Senate seat to Cabinet post in new administration.

CAREER U.S. SENATOR

1881

January 6-17	Indiana Legislature considered senatorial candidates; on 18th ballot cast a majority for Harrison.
January 22	Visited President-elect Garfield at Mentor; renewed preference to take Senate seat rather than place in Cabinet.
March 4	Sworn in as U.S. Senator in a body that counted 37 Democrats, 37 Republicans and 2 Independents.
May 20	Adjournment of Senate; appointed to four committees and chaired Transportation Committee.
July 2	Garfield shot by assassin; joined bedside vigil in White House.
September 20	Death of Garfield reported to Harrison in Chicago; attended funeral in D.C. and interment in Cleveland.
October 10-24	Made first two speeches in Senate.
November	Attended Battle of Yorktown centennial in Virginia.

1882

March	Voted to establish nine-man Tariff Commission; yet maintained protectionist views in 47th and succeeding Congresses.
March-April	Voted against exclusion of Chinese from West Coast. Bill passed and vetoed by President Arthur. Veto upheld.
April	Spoke against federal spending on "The Levee Question"; accused by Southern Senators of "waving bloody shirt."

August 29   Advocated civil service reform; supported move to pass Pendleton Bill.

1883

September   Campaigned vigorously in Iowa and Ohio; stressed "bloody shirt," tariff and civil rights issues.

October   Assailed Supreme Court ruling against equal rights for Negroes.

October 16   Praised by Senator William Boyd Allison.

1884

January 1   In letter to Wharton Barker denied any presidential ambition; affirmed support for protective tariff and opposition to free whiskey.

January 9   Marriage of son, Russell, to May Saunders, daughter of Nebraska Senator, Alvin P. Saunders. Attended ceremony in Trinity Cathedral at Omaha.

January 15   Spoke at unveiling of Oliver P. Morton's statue, now an Indianapolis landmark. Suggested erection of monument to all Hoosier servicemen, thus initiating present 285-foot shaft in Monument Circle.

April   Accepted post of delegate-at-large to Republican National Convention to meet in Chicago in June.

May   Introduced bill to provide civil government for Alaska; passed House on May 13; pushed efforts to give Washington, Montana, Wyoming statehood.

June 3-6   8th Republican National Convention; role as "favorite son" resulted in return to Indianapolis; Indiana supported Blaine who won nomination on fourth ballot.

June 19   In Washington, D.C. delivered keynote for Blaine at party ratification ceremonies.

August 21	Asked by Blaine to institute libel suit against Indianapolis *Sentinel*: took case under advisement.
August 23	Opened national campaign in Indianapolis.
August 30–September 5	Took stump for Blaine in Maine, making five speeches and spending weekend with candidate in Augusta.
October	Blaine dropped libel suit, thus freeing Harrison for campaign appearances.
November 4	Election of President Grover Cleveland.
November 5	Marriage of daughter, Mamie, to Robert McKee in Indianapolis.
November 21	Wharton Barker's letter to Harrison: "Great power rests in your hands . . . The Republican Party will follow you."
December 25	Spent Christmas in Washington; studied naval bill and history of the Monroe Doctrine.

1885

January–February	Preferred Interstate Commerce Commission plan over Reagan Bill to correct railroad abuses; Interstate Act became law in 1887; attacked Cleveland's position on silver; opposed Cabinet members Manning and Whitney as "monopolists."
March	Appointed chairman of Military Committee.
March 5	Embittered by Indiana reapportionment law as unfair to GOP.
May 5	Opened campaign of 1886 to counteract gerrymander and to secure own re-election.
July–August	Six weeks trip to Pacific Coast to conduct en route investigation for sub-committee on Indian Affairs.

October	Campaigned for re-election of Senator John Sherman of Ohio.
December	Attacked Administration for abuses of civil service reform and unfair treatment of ex-soldiers.

1886

January-February	Harrison's Dakota Bill passed by Senate only after a bitterly partisan debate.
Spring	Fought for pensions, health laws and capital-labor reforms; led battle on Tenure of Office Act.
May 7	Ohio Society of New York invited him as principal speaker; press reported him "very much a leader of men."
August 5	Congress adjourned. Indiana state campaign got under way.
September-October	Spoke in almost every county; helped write GOP state platform.
November 5	Republicans won small victory, just 7 out of 13 congressional seats; own re-election to Senate in doubt.
December 6	Returned to D.C. for 2nd session of 49th Congress; spent Christmas recess in Indianapolis.

1887

February	Vote of Indiana Legislature on 16th ballot made Harrison's second term as Senator impossible. Democrat David Turpie elected to succeed him.
February 11	Spoke to Young Republicans at Providence, Rhode Island.
February 12	Called for "Reform of the Party within the Party" at Lincoln Day dinner in New York.
March 3	Left U.S. Senate.
March 15	Given grandson by daughter, Mamie McKee, who called him (future Baby McKee) Benjamin Harrison McKee.

June-July   Won verdict and substantial fee in Wise will case at Sullivan, Indiana.

August   Vacationed at Deer Park, Maryland. Political conferences result in talk of running him for President in 1888, especially if Blaine should step aside; assured by Davis and Elkins that as "citizen-soldier" he was "presidential timber."

December 6   Cleveland's Free Trade message to Congress affords GOP an issue for next presidential campaign.

CAMPAIGN FOR PRESIDENCY

1888

January 18   Granddaughter, Marthena Harrison, born in Omaha.

January 25   From Florence, Italy, Blaine formally withdraws name from '88 race.

February 12 Elkins said Harrison was Blaine's heir as party leader.

February 22 At Detroit (annual Michigan Club banquet) broke political silence, claiming self as "a living and rejuvenated Republican." Attracted national attention.

March 20   At Chicago (Marquette Club) lauded as candidate with "head full of brains . . . born fighter" and party's hope "against the Democracy, the flesh and the devil."

April-May   Sentiment for Harrison crystallized on a national scale.

June 19-23, 25 At Civic Auditorium, Chicago, Illinois, 9th GOP Convention, on 8th ballot, named Harrison for presidency and Levi P. Morton (New York) for vice-presidency.

July 4   Officially notified of nomination at Indianapolis home; accepted engrossed copy of platform.

July 13-August 4 Lew Wallace dictated campaign biography entitled: "Life of Ben Harrison by the Author of Ben Hur." Published, September 1.

July 7-   Delivered over eighty *ex tempore* campaign speeches to
October 25   nearly 300,000 people who came to Indianapolis. Most celebrated "Front-Porch" campaign to date.

August 17   Organization of the Harrison Marching Club (today the
                Columbia Club of Indianapolis).

August 21   Ended first phase of personal campaign that began July 7;
                stressed Americanism, protection to labor, social order,
                and to veterans by pensions; attacked "combinations of
                trusts and civil service abuses."

August 21-   Respite near Put-in-Bay Island, Lake Erie, where Oliver
Labor Day   Hazard Perry won celebrated battle over British fleet.

September 12   Published formal Letter of Acceptance that evoked partisan
                plaudits.

September 14-   Second phase of campaign, made forty speeches to 20,000
October 25   who crowded into Indianapolis.

October 11   Blaine addressed 75,000 in Indianapolis; 25,000 marchers
                evaluated by A.P. as probably the greatest political parade
                ever witnessed . . . outside the city of New York."

October 25   Repudiated "dollar a day" tag as bigoted lie; reaffirmed
                support of high tariff to protect American labor. Probably
                most influential speech of entire campaign.

October 25-   Final fortnight of contest styled by Albert J. Beveridge as
November 8   struggle between "Beef" Cleveland and "Brains" Harrison.

October 31   "Blocks of Five" scandal hit Indianapolis; denied by
                alleged author, W.W. Dudley as forgery; silence main-
                tained by presidential candidate.

November 6-   Trailed Cleveland by over 90,000 votes, yet won by an
Election Day   electoral count of 233 to 168. Received 58.1 percent (20
                states) as compared to Cleveland's 41.9 percent (18 states).

November 9   Democratic National Chairman Calvin S. Brice sent con-
                gratulations: "You have made a great race and won the
                greatest prize on this earth. I do not mean the Presidency
                merely but the Presidency—worthy to have it and worthily
                won."

December   Visited by GOP National Chairman Matthew Quay who
                reported President-elect attributed victory to Providence.
                Quay said later: "Providence hadn't a damn thing to do
                with it."

1889

January 1   Open house reception for nearly 2,000 neighbors.

January 17   Invited Blaine to be Secretary of State and cornerstone of Cabinet that Harrison would name and publish only after Inauguration.

February 25   Departed Indianapolis for Washington, telling crowd at station: "There is a great sense of loneliness in the discharge of high public duties. The moment of decision is one of isolation."

March 1   Completed draft of Inaugural address; read same to Senators John Sherman and George Edmunds, as well as to future Cabinet members James Blaine and William Windom.

March 2   Visited Cleveland in White House; reciprocated by outgoing President same afternoon. Cordiality prevailed.

TERM OF OFFICE

March 4   Inaugurated 23rd President on Monday in the rain. Chief Justice Melville W. Fuller administered the oath of office on family Bible. A lengthy Inaugural called for American growth in a more perfect Union in which free men could enjoy material prosperity without special regard for sectionalism. He pledged social justice for all men and promised early statehood for territories, a free ballot for Negroes, pensions for veterans. A promise to enforce the civil service law irked spoilsmen. He stated that foreign policy would be vigilant of national honor and would protect the commercial and personal rights of Americans everywhere. In stressing the essentials of the Monroe Doctrine, he urged building a modern navy and merchant marine. He pledged noninterference in the affairs of foreign governments and favored arbitration of international quarrels as a move toward world peace. Yet he put national strength first and foremost.

     In naming his own Cabinet, Harrison gave party managers little or no say. Only one of eight worked for Harrison at the convention. In summary he leaned with conviction toward age and experience. Only Attorney General William Henry Harrison Miller (a law partner) and Postmaster

General John Wanamaker were younger than the President. Secretary of the Treasury William Windom, 61, ranked as senior member, Secretary of State James G. Blaine, 59, came next. Secretary of War Redfield Proctor, Secretary of Navy Benjamin Tracy, and Secretary of Agriculture Jeremiah Rusk admitted to be 58, and Interior Secretary John W. Noble was 57.

March 7   First Cabinet meeting; decided against kitchen Cabinet and attacked spoils system and "senatorial courtesy."

April 22   Oklahoma opened to settlers; overnight Guthrie had nearly 10,000, within six months the Territory had 29 schools, 38 churches, and 22 newspapers.

April 29   Berlin Conference on Samoan affairs began.

April 29-
May 1   Central figure in Centennial celebration in New York to commemorate Washington's First Inauguration; initiated crusade to fly American flag over every schoolhouse.

May 3-7   Invited Theodore Roosevelt to White House; appointed him Civil Service Commissioner.

May 31   Johnstown flood. Sent federal aid and addressed public fund-raising dinner in D.C.

June 19, 26   Accepted honorary degrees of doctor of laws from Princeton and alma mater, Miami University.

July-
August 30   Rented summer White House at Deer Park, Maryland; often commuted to Washington.

August 6-15   Interrupted vacation to visit Blaine in Maine; toured New England; revealed plans for expanded merchant marine and two-ocean navy.

August 14   Deputy U.S. Marshal David Neagle shot and killed Judge David Terry who attempted to assassinate Supreme Court Justice Stephen J. Field. President brought case to attention of Congress; Supreme Court sustained President as the principal conservator "of the peace of the United States" (*In re Neagle*, 133 U.S. 1, 59 (1890) on April 14.

August 22   Dedicated Sailors' and Soldiers' Monument in Indianapolis.

October 2	Pan-American Conference. Arranged the election of Blaine as chairman of the Congress; 70 business meetings held; adjournment on April 19, 1890. Harrison praised by press: "From this day the Monroe Doctrine passes by process of diplomatic evolution into stage of higher development."
November 2	North and South Dakota admitted as 39th and 40th states; first instance of twin states entering Union at same moment.
November 8	Montana became 41st state.
November 11	Washington became 42nd state.
December 2	Election of "Czar" Thomas B. Reed as Speaker of the House.
December 3	Sent first message to Congress; recommended pensions for veterans, civil service reform, civil rights, improved conditions for railroad workers, and naval legislation.
December 4	Nominated David J. Brewer, 52, to be Associate Justice of Supreme Court. Confirmed two weeks later by Senate.
December 6	Death of Jefferson Davis.
December 8	Dedicated Chicago Auditorium (now Roosevelt University).
December 25	White House mourns deaths of sister-in-law, Elizabeth Scott Lord and nephew, William Sheets Harrison.

1890

January 15	Death of Walker Blaine, first son of Secretary of State; daughter Alice Coppinger died few days later.
February 3	Navy Secretary Tracy's home ravaged by fire that proved fatal to Mrs. Tracy, daughter, Mary, and a maid. Harrison administered artificial respiration to Tracy, helping to save his life; afforded deceased a White House funeral and welcomed bereaved Secretary into family circle at Executive Mansion.
June	Pension Bill became law, thus giving legal precedent to the principle of service pensions to provide for minors,

dependent parents and widows of old soldiers. By 1907 the law cost the government over a billion dollars.

July 2   Sherman Anti-Trust Act enacted; House passed Force Bill to guarantee Negro voting rights; Senate action delayed.

July 3   Idaho admitted as 43rd state.

July 10   Wyoming became 44th state.

July 14   Sherman Silver Purchase Act signed into law by Harrison who personally convinced free silver senators to the compromise. Aided by "Czar" Reed.

July-August   Extensive White House renovation; Wanamaker cottage at Cape May, New Jersey, presented to Mrs. Harrison. Bought by President; served as summer White House; sold by Harrison in 1896 for original purchase price of $10,000. Criticized as "Gift Grabber" in 1890.

July 29   Special Message to Congress requesting legislation to ban lottery ticket sales by mail.

August 11   Addressed G.A.R. National Encampment at Boston.

August 16   House passed stringent anti-lottery bill; two weeks later Senate concurred.

September 13-18 Tight money crisis on Wall Street averted by Harrison and Treasury Secretary Windom.

September 19 Anti-Lottery Act signed into law.

October 1   51st Congress adjourned; dubbed as "The Billion Dollar Congress"; passed a record number of bills during historic first session. McKinley Tariff and Reciprocity Act, passed by Senate on September 10, signed into law. Became off-year election issue. McKinley Tariff and Reciprocity Act, passed by Senate on September 10, signed into law. Became off-year election issue.

October 6-13 Made campaign tour of Midwest that covered 3,000 miles and called for more than 40 speeches.

November 7   Elections resulted in Democratic sweep of House; GOP Senate majority reduced to 8.

December 1   Second annual message to Congress.

December 29   Promoted Judge Henry B. Brown to Supreme Court.

1891

January 29   Sudden death of Treasury Secretary Windom.

February 14   Deaths of Admiral David Porter and General William T. Sherman.

February 23   Charles Foster of Ohio named to Treasury.

February 28   Signed historic measure creating Circuit Court of Appeals.

March 14   New Orleans lynching incident; Italy severs diplomatic ties with U.S.; war threatened; Mafia blamed; affair settled only in 1892 — by indemnity payment.

April 14-
May 21   Presidential speaking tour to the South and Pacific Coast — a round trip of 9,232 miles; made 140 impromptu speeches. Another presidential first!

May 6   *Itata* incident — an alleged violation of U.S. neutrality by Chilean revolutionaries — set stage for war fever.

May 22, 23   Blaine desperately ill; long convalescence followed.

June   Signed several new reciprocity agreements.

July-August   Summer vacation at Cape May.

September 16   White House refurbished.

October 16   Sailors from U.S.S. *Baltimore* on shore leave in Valparaiso attacked by Chilean rioters. Two killed, 17 others injured. War scare increased.

December 9   Annual message to Congress styled the attack as "savage, brutal, unprovoked."

December 16   Nominated Stephen B. Elkins as new Secretary of War.

December 25   Tense Christmas at White House. Foresaw war with Chile;
                   denied desire for renomination.

                                   1892

January 1-20   "The President stated all members of Cabinet are for
                   War," but Blaine advised against an ultimatum.

January 20   Chile demanded recall of U.S. Minister Patrick Egan.

January 21   U.S. sent ultimatum to Chile.

January 25   Special message to Congress asks "appropriate action."

January 26   Chile backed down; ultimately paid indemnity of $75,000.

April-May   Wife confined to bed; diagnosis was nervous prostration.

May 7   Son, Russell, angered Blaine; relations between Secretary
                   and President deteriorate.

May   Laid cornerstone for Grant's Tomb on Riverside Drive,
                   New York.

May 23   Decided to fight for renomination, saying: "No Harrison
                   has ever retreated in the presence of a foe without giving
                   battle." Opposed by party bosses; hostility of Blaine
                   deepened.

June 4   Resignation of Blaine three days before National Con-
                   vention. Accepted immediately.

June 7-10   10th GOP National Convention at Minneapolis. Nominated
                   on first ballot, getting 904 votes with 453 necessary for
                   nomination. Nominated for Vice President — Whitelaw
                   Reid, New York.

June 20   Harrison notified officially in D.C.

June 22   Democratic National Convention in Chicago nominated
                   Grover Cleveland and Adlai E. Stevenson, Illinois.

July 4   Populist party named General James B. Weaver for Presi-
                   dent on third party ticket.

July 6   Tragedy at Homestead Works of the Carnegie Steel Company near Pittsburgh. Twenty killed in a battle between locked-out workers and armed Pinkerton emissaries.

July 12   Violent strike by silver miners at Coeur d'Alene, Idaho, 30 fell dead as miners fought non-union help. Harrison sent federal troops to restore order.

July 13   Addressed National Educational Association in Saratoga; stressed need for law and order.

July 26   Appointed Judge George Shiras, Jr. of Pittsburgh, Associate Justice of the Supreme Court.

July 30   Privately supported mediation of Homestead strike; asked Whitelaw Reid to send emissary to Henry Clay Frick; no tangible results; strike lasted five months and broke union, known as Amalgamated Association of Iron and Steel Workers; organized labor set back nearly a half-century.

July-September Mrs. Harrison, suffering from tuberculosis, taken to Loon Lake, a quiet Adirondack village in northern New York. President did not campaign; commuted from Washington until Congress quit in August.

September 21 Wife brought home to White House to die. Month of bedside vigils ensued.

October 25 Death came peacefully. White House funeral with burial in Indianapolis.

November 8 Defeated by Grover Cleveland in national election; trailed in popular vote by nearly 380,000 out of 10 million; lost in electoral college. Cleveland 62.39 percent (277 votes—23 states); Harrison got 32.66 percent (145 votes—16 states); Weaver—4.95 percent (22 votes—4 states).

1893

January   Traditional receptions cancelled as mourning period for Mrs. Harrison continued; scarlet fever strikes White House, impairing granddaughter Marthena Harrison. With the deaths of former President Hayes and ex-Secretary Blaine, the number of fatalities connected with the Administration reached a record of twenty.

January 29   News of Hawaiian revolt reached Washington.

February 16   Sent treaty to Senate, asking for Hawaiian "annexation, full and complete." Badly divided Senate refused to act.

February 18   Nominated Federal Judge Howell E. Jackson, a Tennessee Democrat, to be Associate Justice of the Supreme Court.

March 4   Attended Cleveland's Inauguration and returned to Indianapolis.

RETIREMENT YEARS (1893-1901)

1893

Summer   At Cape May, New Jersey, began preparation of six law lectures to be delivered at Stanford University in 1894.

September 1-7   Presided at G.A.R. Encampment held in Indianapolis.

Fall and Winter   Declined endowed professorship at University of Chicago, as well as offer to become a bank president, to resume lucrative legal practice.

December 22   Addressed New England Society of Pennsylvania at Philadelphia. Later published as a chapter in *Views of an Ex-President*.

1894

Spring   Took daughter and grandchildren to West Coast; delivered law lectures at Stanford. Later revised them for publication.

Summer   Vacationed at Monmouth Beach, New Jersey; mostly avoided politics and out-of-state campaigns.

September   Delivered twenty speeches in Indiana canvass.

October   Spoke at Carnegie Hall (New York) to help former Vice-President Morton win governorship. During address was sketched by Canadian artist, John Colin Forbes.

November 7   Hailed Morton's and GOP victory as happy cyclone and landslide.

1895

January-May	Gained verdict in celebrated Morrison Will case at Richmond, Indiana. Accepted fee of $25,000.
March	First serious illness — two-week bout with "la grippe."
Late Spring	Sat for official White House portrait at Eastman Johnson Studios in New York.
June 10	Appointed trustee of Purdue University.
Summer	First Adirondack vacation at Old Forge, New York; later purchased camp he called "Berkeley Lodge" after Virginia plantation of Governor Benjamin Harrison V, the great-grandfather who signed the Declaration of Independence.
Winter	During Christmas season announced engagement to widow, Mary Lord Dimmick, daughter of the first Mrs. Harrison's sister. Income estimated at $50,000 was derived from law practice, writing, lecturing and investments.

1896

February 3	Publicly declined to be GOP candidate for President.
April 27	Second marriage at St. Thomas's Episcopal Church in New York City. Former Navy Secretary B.F. Tracy was best man; most ex-members of Cabinet attended, as did then Governor Levi P. Morton, former Vice President.
May-June	Talk of another presidential candidacy refused to die after two years. Old ticket of 1888 "Harrison and Morton" boomed.
June 16-18	National Convention at St. Louis nominated William McKinley on first ballot. Harrison avoided preconvention squabbles by noninvolvement policy.
July-August	Vacation at Berkeley Lodge. Continued work on nine articles (about 3,000 words each) on the machinery of national government. Publication in the *Ladies' Home Journal* won wide acclaim.

August 27 At Carnegie Hall launched national campaign to elect McKinley. Keynote address refuted free silver and stressed need for protective tariff. *Ex tempore* speech praised by John Hay for "splendor of diction" and "mastery of method."

September Campaigned in Virginia, West Virginia and Ohio. Said William Jennings Bryan was politically dead.

October Made 40 speeches in Indiana.

November 3 McKinley elected. Harrison retired from active politics.

1897

February 21 At 63 became father of Elizabeth, one of the few children to be born of an ex-President. Daughter named after his mother and wife's grandmother.

March 23 Address at University of Michigan on "Some Hindrances to Law Reforms."

Summer Declined all further speaking invitations, including overtures from American Bar Association and National Education Association. Refused all-expense-paid trips to Europe and Japan.

Published *This Country of Ours.* Enjoyed wide sale in U.S., Europe and South America. Translated into five foreign languages.

Fall Abundant legal retainers; cases appellate and federal in nature, involving libel, patent, railroad and tax matters. Argued Illinois Inheritance Tax Cases before U.S. Supreme Court early in 1898.

December First approached by Venezuelan government to act as chief counsel in that country's boundary dispute with British Guiana (now independent Guyana).

1898

January Accepted Venezuela's offer, stipulating a retainer of $20,000 and a total fee of $100,000 for himself and somewhat lesser fees for associate counsel.

March 15   Agreed date for printed case, with December 15, 1898 as date for printed counter-case and summer 1899 as time for oral arguments before Arbitral tribunal in Paris.

April 30   Admiral Dewey took Manila Bay.

May 3   Called Spanish American War "war for humanity . . . for the oppressed of another race. We could not escape this conflict. Spanish rule has become effete. We dare not say that we have God's commission to deliver the oppressed the world around." Son Russell accepted commission as Major and sailed to Cuba.

July 1   Storming of San Juan Hill in Cuba.

July 17   Surrender of Santiago.

August 13   Capture of Manila.

Summer   Refused all other legal employment; devoted full time to Venezuelan case in Indianapolis and in Adirondack hideaway.

December 10   Treaty of Paris signed; Cuba gained independence. Ratified by U.S. Senate in February, 1899, by a vote of 57 to 27.

1899

February 27   Venezuelan case and counter-case completed.

March 1   Death of Lord Herschell delayed oral argument of Boundary Dispute in Paris.

May   Took short rest at Hot Springs, Virginia.

May 17   Sailed for Europe on American liner *St. Paul.*

June 15   International Arbitration Tribunal convened in Paris; sessions lasted until late September.

July 4   In Paris addressed American Chamber of Commerce on recent Spanish American War. Defended U.S. foreign policy as humanitarian rather than colonial, deplored use of arms in settling international questions; repeated conviction that America had no commission to police the world.

September 21-27 Made five-day oral argument (25 hours) in behalf of Venezuela.

October 3   Tribunal's decision disappointed American counsel.

October 4-6   Visited Cologne and Berlin before touring Belgium and England; prompt return voyage to New York.

1900

April 19   As honorary chairman gave opening address to Ecumenical Missionary Conference at Carnegie Hall, New York.

April 21   At same conference gave response to welcoming speeches by President McKinley and Governor Theodore Roosevelt.

May 1   Closed conference with "Farewell Address."

May 6-30   With family, toured Yellowstone Park and the Northwest; did not attend GOP National Convention.

June-September Vacationed in Adirondacks.

August 29   Accepted presidential appointment to the International Court.

December 31   Celebrated address to Columbia Club, Indianapolis—"Hail Columbia—A Land—A Song—A Club."

1901

February 8   Advised Associate Supreme Court Justice Harlan that "the grip" had been knocking at his door; cancelled trip to Washington.

March 3-9   Severe cold developed into pneumonia.

March 13   Died quietly in the arms of his wife.

March 17   Buried in Crown Hill Cemetery, Indianapolis, alongside the first Mrs. Harrison. President McKinley headed the nation's mourners; Hoosier poet James Whitcomb Riley delivered the eulogy.

DOCUMENTS

BENJAMIN HARRISON ON THE STRUGGLES FACED
BY A BRIEFLESS BARRISTER AND A
YOUTHFUL FAMILY MAN
at Indianapolis in 1854

*Harrison's first child, named Russell, was born
August 12, 1854, just eight days before Ben's twenty-
first birthday. Wife and baby stayed with relatives in
Ohio until the fall. The young lawyer remained in
Indianapolis then in the throes of a financial panic.
This fact, coupled with his wife's absence, accentuated
his low spirits. Fortunately, there are preserved two
letters never intended for the public eye. Both, how-
ever, mirror a future President's heart-guarded secrets.
With appropriate editing, they read:*

September 19, 1854

My dear wife,

. . . I feel lonesome . . . (so) I must bind myself more closely to my
books and then I shall feel the want of company less.

. . . You do not know how disheartened I feel sometimes, at the
prospect of sitting in my office, for long months, without getting anything to do. I know I should feel contented if I only had some business
to occupy my attention, however trifling the profits might be. Indeed I
would almost be willing to work for nothing, just for the sake of being
busy. But however much I may be discouraged at the prospect, I never
suffer myself to falter in my purpose—I have long since made up my
mind that with God's blessing and good health *I would* succeed, and I
never allow myself to doubt the result.

It is a great relief in these seasons of depression to have your society,
and I long very much for it now but it seems better that you should

remain where you are, for a season. I hope our place will soon become healthy. Much love to all the family and kisses for the babe.

Your affectionate husband,

P.S. . . . love to all. Write often and let us know how you and the babe get along. I had a bad dream about him last night.

January 5, 1855

Dear Carrie,

. . . I forgot to tell you to write often, but I suppose you will not need the caution. I know you and the babe will be cared for, both at the Point and at Oxford, but as no one loves you as I do, so no one will take as good care of you as I would . . . I wish I were able to send you some money as you should have your teeth fixed etc., but I am now reduced to two dollars myself. I will try to send you some in a day or two, though I am sure I have no idea where it is to come from.

Sid Mear's party I am told is to come off Wednesday. Nothing of interest has transpired since you left. Take good care of our sweet boy and of yourself also. Say to Irwin that if he will bring you out I will not go down, as money is too scarce to be squandered un-necessarily. I would like very much to visit Oxford and will do so if funds are more plenty. If Irwin is coming out however it would be as well for you to come with him. Love to all.

HARRISON THREW IN HIS LOT WITH THE
INSURGENT REPUBLICAN PARTY IN 1856

Harrison lived in politically changing times that saw the disintegration of old political parties and the emergence of a new alignment. He favored the "young Republican colt, a cross with Whig, American, anti-slavery and temperance strains." He thus broke with the beliefs of grandfather William Henry Harrison and father John Scott Harrison by campaigning actively for Republican presidential nominee, John C. Fremont. This step shocked the conservatism of his family but young Harrison worked for the Republican cause until 1860 when he ran for Supreme Court Reporter. In 1860 he spoke out against "slave oligarchy" and "slave aristocracy." His evaluation of Abraham Lincoln is cited below.

Before us stood our chosen leader, the man who was to be our pilot through seas more stormy and through channels more perilous than ever the old ship went before. He had piloted the lumbering flat-boat on our western streams, but he was now to take the helm of the great ship. His experience in public office had been brief, and not conspicuous. He had no general acquaintance with the people of the whole country. His large angular frame and face, his broad humor, his homely illustrations and simple ways, seemed to very many of his fellow-countrymen to portray a man and a mind that, while acute and powerful, had not that nice balance and touch of statecraft that the perilous way before us demanded. No college of arts had opened to his struggling youth; he had been born in a cabin and reared among the unlettered. He was a rail-splitter, a flatboatman, a country lawyer . . . The course before him was lighted only by the lamp of duty; outside its radiance all was dark. He seemed to me to be conscious of all this, to be weighted by it, but so strong was his sense of duty, so courageous his heart, so sure was he of his own high purposes and motives and of the favor of God for himself and his people, that he moved forward calmly to his appointed work; not with show and brag, neither with shrinking.

HARRISON DURING THE CIVIL WAR

*On June 28, 1862 Indiana Governor O.P. Morton
advised President Lincoln that Indiana would respond
to the call for Union reinforcements. On July 9 Harrison volunteered to raise a regiment, drill it, and
move to the front "with a knapsack on his back and a
musket in his hand." Below are two contemporary
newspaper accounts of Harrison's efforts to enlist
recruits.*

July 14, 1862. Benjamin Harrison, Esq., Reporter of the Supreme
Court, said that his determination to volunteer was the result of deliber-
ate judgment. He had calculated the cost and though the sacrifices to
him were great, both in a personal and a business point of view, he had
determined to take the step and he would keep his word. He could not
weigh the questions of profit or tender ties of home against the duty he
owed his Government. And he had no more interest in the country than
any of those to whom he was speaking, and it came home to all. He
trusted many would give their names now, and that their example
would work a good leaven in the hearts of his hearers that would make
it uncomfortable for those who can go to remain at home.

July 18, 1862. Boys, think quick, and decide as patriots should in such
an emergency. Fathers, cease to restrain the ardor of your sons, whose
patriotic impulses prompt them to aid our country in its hour of trials.
Ladies, give the stout and hearty young men who have caught your
smiles, to understand that "the brave alone deserve the fair."

*On August 21, 1862, from the Kentucky front, Har-
rison first wrote to his wife:*

We are proud of her (Indiana) and hope to make her proud of us
before we return from the war. I hope you all remember us at home
and that many prayers go up to God daily for my Regiment and for me.
Ask Him for me in prayer, my dear wife, first that He will enable me
to bear myself as a good soldier of Jesus Christ; second, that He will
give me valor and skill to conduct myself so as to honor my country
and my friends; and lastly, if consistent with His holy will, I may be
brought 'home again' to the dear loved ones, if not, that the rich consolation of His grace may be made sufficient for me and for those who
survive . . . We will improve the time of our stay . . . and be better
prepared to render effective service when called upon.

*On Christmas eve, 1862, Harrison wrote to his wife
a characteristic letter.*

. . . And this is Christmas eve; and the dear little ones are about this time nestling their little heads upon the pillow, filled with the high expectations of what Santa Claus will bring them, and Papa is not there. How sad and trying it is for me to be away at such a time as this, and yet I cannot allow my complaining spirit to possess me. There are tens of thousands of fathers separated like me from the dear ones at home, battling with us for the preservation of our noble government which, under God, has given us all that peace and prosperity which makes our homes abodes of comfort and security. I am enduring very heavy trials in the army, but I believe that I was led to enter it by a high sense of Christian patriotism and God has thus far strengthened me to bear all cheerfully. I can never be too thankful for the heroic spirit with which you bear our separation and its incident trials and hardships. I know you must be very lonesome and oppressed with many anxieties, but God will give you enough strength to bear them all and will, nay I believe already has, drawn you closer to Himself as the source of all comfort and consolation. It is a blessed promise that *"all things* shall work together for good to those who love God." Let us have faith to receive the promise in all its *royal* fulness.

*At war's end, while awaiting the Grand Review in
Washington and official discharge, Harrison wrote to
his wife on April 20.*

. . . I found a most cordial welcome here both from my superiors and inferiors and was compelled to make them a little speech last night. They all expressed the most cordial feeling and the most enthusiastic gladness at my return. It was very gratifying to know that they missed me, and also to be assured that they all gave me credit for a desire to get back. Sherman has completed the terms with Johnston which, if ratified at Washington, will, he says, bring peace from the Potomac to the Rio Grande. And in the meantime we have a suspension of hostilities. We are fixing upon a camp for a stay of ten days or two weeks, and then we expect to march toward home. Yes!, thank God, towards *home*, our work done, our country saved. There is some talk that a portion of the army will march to the Potomac . . . and part back through Georgia. Which way we may go I cannot tell, but I hope towards the East, as I have no fancy for a Georgia trip. My impression is that the Regiments that came out when we did, will be mustered out by the first of June, and that the Colored Troops, the Regulars and the Veterans will be kept as Garrisons for such places as they may think necessary to garrison. It is a most joyous anticipation and I pray nothing may happen to dash our cup of joy.

His final letter of May 21, 1865 served as a treasured blueprint for Mrs. Harrison.

. . . you do not seem willing of late to give me credit for the affection I do really feel for you and our home, but if you could read my heart you would be satisfied that I do not speak half that I feel, and that no object of ambition or gain could ever lead me away from the side of my dear wife and children. I have no doubt from intimations I have received that I could go to Congress for our District at the next election, but positively I would not accept the office, for the reason that it would take me away from home so much. If my ambition is to soar anymore after I come home, you will have to give it wings, for I certainly long only for a life of quiet usefulness at home. You do not know how much I have thought since I left you last as to how I might make my home brighter and happier for you and the children. It has been in my mind on the march, on my cot, and even in my dreams. I know I have the best intentions and the strongest resolutions to devote myself more to your happiness than I have ever done since our marriage, and if I should fail, if you will meet my failure with a kind reminder of what I have promised, I have a good hope that every asperity may be banished from our family intercourse and that we may always express in our lives the devoted affection which I know we have for each other and must have till death parts us. I know you love me Carrie, with more devotion than most women are capable of, and I, so far as my heart or person are worth your acceptance, have given them all to you. Why then should we allow a word or thought or act to express any other feeling. I wish you could give me some little article of apparel or ornament that might always be before my eyes to remind me of the resolutions and vows I have made but I think I have a better idea still, I will bring you a little keepsake when I come home from the war which you shall *always* wear, never putting it off til death shall separate us. And when I deliver it to you we will weave a spell about it that I shall make it to me a constant reminder of the resolutions and vows I have made in the army. Will you wear it and promise me always to hold it up before me when you see a cloud on my brow or hear hasty words from my lips? I have a good hope that by mutual help and by God's help, we may live the residue of our lives without having our hearts' sunshine clouded by a single shade of mistrust or anger. I know it is possible and I would rather succeed in such an effort than to have the highest honors of earth.

HARRISON EMERGES AS A NATIONAL
POLITICAL FIGURE

Mid-way through the 1876 race for the governorship of Indiana Harrison was drafted to replace Republican nominee G. S. Orth. Despite failure to win the contest, his political star ascended until it shone over the White House in 1889. For an understanding of the future President's political views and the development of his philosophy of public life, this segment contains a series of documents that will serve to illustrate his road to the White House. Edited versions are used in the interest of brevity; omitted phrases or sentences are noted by the customary ellipses. Prefatory notes identify issues and background.

August 18, 1876, at Danville, Indiana, gubernatorial candidate Harrison delivered a two-hour speech that set the tone for his entire campaign. On Greenbackism he said that the greenback is a promise by the government to pay money. It says: "The U.S. will pay the bearer one dollar or five dollars." It is the same, declared Harrison, "as if I had your note in which you promised to pay me so much money: 'I promise to pay Benjamin Harrison,' so much money . . . I understand there are some people now who would have what they promised to pay wiped out. Instead of 'United States will pay one dollar,' they would have the government print upon its notes, 'This is a dollar.' That proposition is well illustrated by the story of the milkman who changed the printing on his tickets, which had been 'Good for one pint of milk,' so as to read: 'This is a pint of milk.' The ticket would not do in the coffee. The pasteboard would not answer for the cream. Our greenback friends refuse to follow their logic to its conclusion." He thundered: "It is clear to my mind that we ought not to entrust this practical work to the rebels who loaded us with the debt of the war, or to their northern allies who have always been the defamers of our national credit." Restore the public credit to what?

"Gentlemen, when the feeble and palsied hand of Buchanan let go its struggling hold on our national finances, a government loan, made to pay the ordinary expenses of the government, was put on the market at 15% discount. Is that the condition of things they wish to restore? . . . Is it not a shame that these fellows, coming right out of rebel congresses and blood-stained rebel armies, should go into a political convention and proclaim themselves the custodians of the nation's honor? They taunt us with our failure to make good our promise to pay the legal tender notes in 1865, right upon the close of the war, and yet they are honeying up to the greenback men at the same time they are denouncing the Republican party for not beginning the resumption the very year the war closed. That was the first year ex-rebels had any interest in our currency, and it may be they felt the failure to resume all the more deeply on that account."

> When taunted by Democrats for waving the "bloody shirt," he replied on August 25, 1876: "For one, I accept the banner of the bloody shirt. I am willing to take as our ensign the tattered, worn-out, old gray shirt, worn by some gallant Union hero, stained with his blood as he gave up his life for his country . . . When they purge their party of the leprosy of secession . . . we will bury the 'bloody shirt' in the grave with the honored corpse who wore it and not before." These words received national as well as state recognition, and throughout the remainder of the campaign the Indianapolis Journal featured them proudly on its masthead. To his old friends, the battle-hardened veterans, the General appealed directly: ". . . I would rather march by your side on the dusty road under the dear flag of our Union, and wear the old army shirt stained with drops of blood, than to do service under the black banner of treason."
> As U. S. Senator (1881-1887) Harrison discussed several issues involving federal spending, a protective tariff, civil service reform, Chinese exclusion, Negro and civil rights, and naval affairs; concerning federal aid to education he favored such help in principle but objected to give-away programs.

. . . there is a giving that pauperizes; there is a giving that enfeebles. It is against that sort of giving that I protest . . . giving should always be so regulated as to save self-respect and awaken in the mind of the recipient a lost faith in his ability to take care of himself. We should carefully avoid that giving which creates a disposition to lean and to expect, which takes the stamina and strength and self-dependence and industry out of men.

On the suppressed Republican vote of the South he noted in 1885:

If any prophet had arisen during the war and had predicted such a condition of things as we now see, he would have been stoned to death without the camp. No soldier would have credited a prophecy which involved the placing of the Rebel who was confronting him in battle over the Pension Office.

The disfranchisement of Republicans in the South is a question, the gravity of which cannot be exaggerated; but what can we do? We may place the U.S. Marshals at the polls, if we ever recover the Presidency again; but it has been demonstrated that local sentiment is such that conviction for any violations of election laws is impossible.

Possibly, if we could unite the North and get control of both Houses of Congress and the Presidency, we might take some steps to deprive the South of representation in Congress and the Electoral College, based upon this suppressed vote.

On partisan removals from office he cited widow De la Hunt's protest against her removal as postmistress on secret charges.

I say to the Government—take your post-office, but not under false pretenses. Do this, and I will utter no word of complaint, however unjust it may appear.

Excuse me, my friends, you who have known me from my childhood and are witnesses of my daily and official life—excuse me if I manifest some feeling over this wrong; I cannot help it. War, with its natural and inevitable results, struck down my husband, my protector and support. It was the act of an open foe on the field of battle; whom I try to forgive; but that the Government, to preserve which he sacrificed his life, should connive with secret enemies and false witnesses to strike down his family without an opportunity of vindication is a national disgrace, and an act too cowardly and base for absolution.

Early in 1888 ex-Senator Harrison spoke frequently on national and international affairs. At Detroit in February and at Chicago in March, 1888, he made two political speeches that marked him as a presidential candidate of prestige and stature.

Before the Marquette Club of Detroit, a social and political organization for young Republicans, he stated his GOP credo that the party that saved the Union in the war years would best furnish national leadership in the late '80's and '90's. In his "I am a living and rejuvenated Republican" address, Harrison spoke of Washington, the Republican:

. . . As Republicans we are fortunate, as has been suggested, in the fact that there is nothing in the history of our party, nothing in the principles that we advocate, to make it impossible for us to gather and to celebrate the birthday of any American who honored or defended his country. We could even unite with our Democratic friends in celebrating the birthday of St. Jackson, because we enter into fellowship with him when we read his story of how by proclamation he put down nullification in South Carolina. We could meet with them to celebrate the birthday of Thomas Jefferson; because there is no note in the immortal Declaration or in the Constitution of our country that is out of harmony with Republicanism. But our Democratic friends are under limitation. They have a short calendar of sense, and they must omit from the history of those whose names are on their calendar the best achievements of their lives. I do not know what the party is preserved for. Its history reminds me of the boulder in the stream of progress, impeding and resisting its onward flow and moving only by the force that it resists.

I want to read a very brief extract from a most notable paper—one that was to-day in the Senate at Washington read from the desk by its presiding officer—the "Farewell Address of Washington"; and while it is true that I cannot quote or find in the writings of Washington anything specifically referring to ballot-box fraud, to tissue ballots, to intimidation, to forged tally-sheets, for the reason that these things had not come in his day to disturb the administration of the Government, yet in the comprehensiveness of the words he uttered, like the comprehensive declarations of the Holy Book, we may find admonition and guidance, and even with reference to a condition of things that his pure mind could have never contemplated. Washington said: "Liberty is indeed little less than a name where the Government is too feeble to withstand the enterprises of factions, to confine each member of society within the limits prescribed by the law, and to maintain all in the secure and tranquil enjoyment of the rights of persons and property." If I had read that to a Democratic meeting they would have suspected that it was an extract from some Republican speech. My countrymen, this Government is that which I love to think of as my country; for not acres, or railroads, or farm products, or bulk meats, or Wall Street, or all combined, are the country that I love. It is the institution, the form of government, the frame of civil society, for which that flag stands, and which we love to-day. It is what Mr. Lincoln so tersely, yet so felicitously, described as a government of the people, by the people, and for the people; a government of the people, because they instituted it—the Constitution reads, "We the people, have ordained"; by the people, because it is in all its departments administered by them; for the people, because it states as its object of supreme attainment the happiness, security and peace of the people that dwell under it.

> *At the conclusion of this address he asked for a remedy against election frauds and disfranchisement of Southern Negroes.*

There is vast power in a protest. Public opinion is the most potent monarch this world knows to-day. Czars tremble in its presence; and we may bring to bear upon this question a public sentiment, by bold and fearless denunciation of it, that will do a great deal towards correcting it. Why, my countrymen, we meet now and then with these Irish-Americans and lift our voices in denunciations of the wrongs which England is perpetrating upon Ireland. We do not elect any Members of Parliament, but the voice of free America protesting against these centuries of wrongs has had a most potent influence in creating, stimulating and sustaining the liberal policy of William E. Gladstone and his associates. Cannot we do as much for oppressed Americans? Can we not make our appeal to these Irish-American citizens who appeal to us in behalf of their oppressed fellow-countrymen to rally with us in this crusade against election frauds and intimidation in the country that they have made their own?

There may be legislative remedies in sight when we can once again possess both branches of the national Congress and have an executive at Washington who has not been created by these crimes against the ballot. Whatever they are, we will seek them out and put them into force—not in a spirit of enmity against the men who fought against us —forgetting the war, but only insisting that now, nearly a quarter of a century after it is over, a free ballot shall not be denied to Republicans in these States where rebels have been rehabilitated with a full citizenship. Every question waits the settlement of this. The tariff question would be settled already if the 1,000,000 of black laborers in the South had their due representation in the House of Representatives.

In the Chicago address (Marquette Club Banquet, March 20, 1888) Harrison explained what the Republican party meant to him in terms of progress and prosperity.

We took the ship of state when there was treachery at the helm, when there was mutiny on the deck, when the ship was among the rocks, and we put loyalty at the helm; we brought the deck into order and subjection. We have brought the ship into the wide and open sea of prosperity, and is it to be suggested that the party that has accomplished these magnificent achievements cannot sail and manage the good ship in the frequented roadways of ordinary commerce? . . .

Defeated once, we are ready for this campaign . . . and I believe that the great party of 1860 is gathering together for the coming election with a force and a zeal and a resolution that will inevitably carry it, under the standard-bearer who may be chosen here in June, to victory in November.

Nominated for the Presidency on June 25, Harrison received the official notification on July 4, 1888. In a gracious speech of acceptance he referred to Independence Day itself:

The day you have chosen for this visit suggests no thoughts that are not in harmony with the occasion. The Republican party has walked in the light of the Declaration of Independence. It has lifted the shaft of patriotism upon the foundation laid at Bunker Hill. It has made the more perfect union secure by making all men free. Washington and Lincoln, Yorktown and Appomattox, the Declaration of Independence and the Proclamation of Emancipation are naturally and worthily associated in our thoughts to-day.

As soon as may be possible I shall by letter communicate to your chairman a more formal acceptance of the nomination, but it may be proper for me now to say that I have already examined the platform with some care, and that its declarations, to some of which your chairman has alluded, are in harmony with my views. It gives me pleasure, gentlemen, to receive you in my home and to thank you for the cordial manner in which you have conveyed your official message.

On departing for Washington at the end of February, President-elect Harrison gave a "Farewell to Indianapolis" address. In part, he noted:

There is a great sense of loneliness in the discharge of high public duties. The moment of decision is one of isolation. But there is One whose help comes even into the quiet chamber of judgment, and to His wise and unfailing guidance will I look for direction and safety. My family unite with me in grateful thanks for this cordial good-bye and with me wish that these years of separation may be full of peace and happiness for each of you.

INAUGURAL ADDRESS
Washington, D.C.
March 4, 1889

*Harrison's Inaugural address was delivered in the
rain. He wore a high silk hat and a Prince Albert coat.
As centennial President he alluded to territorial expansion, and to increases in population and corporate
wealth. He called for greater effort to form a more
perfect Union that surpassed merely sectional interests.
"Laws are general, and their administration should be
uniform and equal," he said. Excerpts below indicate
a concern for Negro voting rights and for social justice
that would thwart the evils of trusts and monopolies.
In foreign affairs he updated the Monroe Doctrine and
promised to build a modern navy. Early statehood for
territories, a free ballot, and a plan to pension war
veterans and their families were advocated. Besides a
pledge to enforce and extend civil service reform, he
asked for more universal education and a deeper
patriotism.*

It is not a departure, but a return that we have witnessed. The
protective policy had then its opponents. The argument was made, as
now, that its benefits inured to particular classes or sections. If the
question became in any sense, or at any time, sectional, it was only
because slavery existed in some of the States. But for this there was no
reason why the cotton producing States should not have led or walked
abreast with the New England States in the production of cotton fabrics.
There was this reason only why the States that divide with Pennsylvania the mineral treasures of the great southeastern and central moun-
tain ranges should have been so tardy in bringing to the smelting
furnace and the mill the coal and iron from their near opposing hillsides.
Mill fires were lighted at the funeral pyre of slavery. The emancipation
proclamation was heard in the depths of the earth as well as in the
sky; men were made free and material things became our better servants.
  Shall the prejudices and paralysis of slavery continue to hang upon
the skirts of progress? How long will those who rejoice that slavery no
longer exists cherish or tolerate the incapacities it puts upon these
communities? I look hopefully to the continuance of our protective
system and to the consequent development of manufacturing and mining
enterprises in the States hitherto wholly given to agriculture as a potent

influence in the perfect unification of our people. The men who have invested their capital in these enterprises, the farmers who have felt the benefit of their neighborhood, and the men who work in shop or field will not fail to find and to defend a community of interest. Is it not quite possible that the farmers and the promoters of the great mining and manufacturing enterprises which have recently been established in the South may yet find that the free ballot of the workingman, without distinction of race, is needed for their defense as well as for his own? I do not doubt that if these men in the South who now accept the tariff views of Clay and the constitutional expositions of Webster would courageously avow and defend their real convictions they would not find it difficult, by friendly instruction and cooperation, to make the black man their efficient and safe ally, not only in establishing correct principles in our national administration, but in preserving for their local communities the benefits of social order and economical and honest government. At least until the good offices of kindness and education have been fairly tried the contrary conclusion cannot be plausibly urged.

If our great corporations would more scrupulously observe their legal obligations and duties, they would have less cause to complain of the unlawful limitations of their rights or of violent interference with their operations. The community that by concert, open or secret, among its citizens, denies to a portion of its members their plain rights under the law, has severed the only safe bond of social order and prosperity. The evil works, from a bad center, both ways. It demoralizes those who practice it, and destroys the faith of those who suffer by it in the efficiency of the law as a safe protector. The man in whose breast that faith has been darkened is naturally the subject of dangerous and uncanny suggestions. Those who use unlawful methods, if moved by no higher motive than the selfishness that prompts them, may well stop and inquire what is to be the end of this. An unlawful expedient can not become a permanent condition of government. If the educated and influential classes in a community either practice or connive at the systematic violation of laws that seem to them to cross their convenience, what can they expect when the lesson that convenience or a supposed class interest is a sufficient cause for lawlessness has been well learned by the ignorant classes? A community where law is the rule of conduct, and where courts, not mobs, execute its penalties, is the only attractive field for business investments and honest labor.

We have not sought to dominate or to absorb any of our weaker neighbors, but rather to aid and encourage them to establish free and stable governments, resting upon the consent of their own people. We have a clear right to expect, therefore, that no European government will seek to establish colonial dependencies upon the territory of these independent American States. That which a sense of justice restrains us from seeking they may be reasonably expected willingly to forego.

It must not be assumed, however, that our interests are so exclusively American that our entire inattention to any events that may transpire elsewhere can be taken for granted. Our citizens domiciled for purposes of trade in all countries and in many of the islands of the sea demand and will have our adequate care in their personal and commercial rights. The necessities of our navy require convenient coaling stations and dock and harbor privileges. These and other trading privileges we will feel free to obtain only by means that do not in any degree partake of coercion, however feeble the Government from which we ask such concessions. But having fairly obtained them by methods, and for purposes entirely consistent with the most friendly disposition toward all other powers, our consent will be necessary to any modification or impairment of the concession.

We shall neither fail to respect the flag of any friendly nation or the just rights of its citizens, nor to exact the like treatment for our own. Calmness, justice, and consideration should characterize our diplomacy. The offices of an intelligent diplomacy or of a friendly arbitration, in proper cases, should be adequate to the peaceful adjustment of all international difficultires. By such methods we will make our contribution to the world's peace, which no nation values more highly, and avoid the opprobrium which must fall upon the nation that ruthlessly breaks it.

Heads of departments, bureaus, and all other public officers having any duty connected therewith, will be expected to enforce the civil service law fully and without evasion. Beyond this obvious duty I hope to do something more to advance the reform of the civil service. The ideal, or even my own ideal, I shall probably not attain. Retrospect will be a safer basis of judgment than promises. We shall not, however, I am sure, be able to put our civil service upon a nonpartisan basis until we have secured an incumbency that fair minded men of the opposition will approve for impartiality and integrity. As the number of such in the civil list is increased removals from office will diminish.

The construction of a sufficient number of modern war ships and of their necessary armament should progress as rapidly as is consistent with care and perfection in plans and workmanship. The spirit, courage, and skill of our naval officers and seamen have many times in our history given to weak ships and inefficient guns a rating greatly beyond that of the naval list. That they will again do so upon occasion I do not doubt; but they ought not, by premeditation or neglect, to be left to the risks and exigencies of an unequal combat.

Our pension law should give more adequate and discriminating relief to the Union soldiers and sailors and to their widows and orphans. Such occasions as this should remind us that we owe everything to their valor and sacrifice.

I do not mistrust the future. Dangers have been in frequent ambush along our path, but we have uncovered and vanquished them all. Passion has swept some of our communities, but only to give us a new demonstration that the great body of our people are stable, patriotic, and law-abiding. No political party can long pursue advantage at the expense of public honor or by rude and indecent methods without protest and fatal disaffection in its own body. The peaceful agencies of commerce are more fully revealing the necessary unity of all our communities, and the increasing intercourse of our people is promoting mutual respect. We shall find unalloyed pleasure in the revelation which our next census will make of the swift development of the great resources of some of the States. Each State will bring its generous contribution to the great aggregate of the nation's increase. And when the harvest from the fields, the cattle from the hills, and the ores of the earth shall have been weighed, counted, and valued, we will turn from them all to crown with the highest honor the State that has most promoted education, virtue, justice, and patriotism among the people.

PROCLAMATION ON
WASHINGTON CENTENNIAL ANNIVERSARY
April 4, 1889

A hundred years have passed since the Government which our fore-fathers founded was formally organized. At noon on the 30th day of April, 1789, in the city of New York, and in the presence of an assemblage of the heroic men whose patriotic devotion had led the colonies to victory and independence, George Washington took the oath of office as Chief Magistrate of the new-born Republic. This impressive act was preceded, at 9 o'clock in the morning, in all the churches of the city, by prayer for God's blessing on the Government and its first President.

The centennial of this illustrious event in our history has been declared a general holiday by act of Congress to the end that the people of the whole country may join in commemorative exercises appropriate to the day.

In order that the joy of the occasion may be associated with a deep thankfulness in the minds of the people for all our blessings in the past, and a devout supplication to God for their gracious continuance in the future, the representatives of the religious creeds, both Christian and Hebrew, have memorialized the Government to designate an hour for prayer and thanksgiving on that day.

Now, therefore, I, Benjamin Harrison, President of the United States of America, in response to this pious and reasonable request, do recommend that on Tuesday, April 30, at the hour of 9 o'clock in the morning, the people of the entire country repair to their respective places of divine worship, to implore the favor of God that the blessings of liberty, prosperity and peace may abide with us as a people, and that His hand may lead us in the paths of righteousness and good deeds.

HARRISON'S TRIBUTE TO WASHINGTON
April 30, 1889

Harrison found himself the central figure at Centennial ceremonies in New York from April 29 to May 1. At New York Subtreasury, April 30, 1889, he made the following speech on the spot where Washington was inaugurated:

Mr. Chairman, my countrymen: Official duty of a very exacting character has made it quite impossible that I should deliver an address on this occasion. Foreseeing this, I early notified your committee that the programme must not contain any address by me. The selection of Mr. Depew as the orator of this occasion makes further speech not only difficult, but superfluous. He has met the demand of this great occasion on its own high level. He has brought before us the incidents and the lessons of the first inauguration of Washington. We seem to have been a part of that admiring and almost adoring throng that filled these streets one hundred years ago.

We have come into the serious, but always inspiring, presence of Washington. He was the incarnation of duty, and he teaches us to-day this great lesson: That those who would associate their names with events that shall outlive a century can only do so by high consecration to duty. Self-seeking has no public observance or anniversary. The captain who gives to the sea his cargo of goods, that he may give safety and deliverance to his imperiled fellowmen, has fame; he who lands the cargo has only wages. Washington seemed to come to the discharge of the duties of his high office impressed with a great sense of his unfamiliarity with these new calls thrust upon him, modestly doubtful of his own ability, but trusting implicitly in the sustaining helpfulness and grace of that God who rules the world, presides in the councils of nations, and is able to supply every human defect. We have made marvelous progress in material things since then, but the stately and enduring shaft that we have erected at the national capital at Washington symbolizes the fact that he is still the First American Citizen.

At the banquet, Metropolitan Opera House, Harrison responded to the toast "The United States of America." This occasion marked the beginning of a presidential crusade to bring increased honor to the American flag.

The occasion and all of its incidents will be memorable not only in the history of your own city, but in the history of our country. New York did not succeed in retaining the seat of National Government here, although she made liberal provision for the assembling of the first Congress in the expectation that the Congress might find its permanent home here. But though you lost that which you coveted, I think the representatives here of all the States will agree that it was fortunate that the first inauguration of Washington took place in the State and city of New York.

For where in our country could the centennial of the event be so worthily celebrated as here? What seaboard offered so magnificent a bay on which to display our merchant and naval marine? What city offered thoroughfares so magnificent, or a people so great, so generous, as New York has poured out to-day to celebrate that event?

I congratulate you to-day, as one of the instructive and interesting features of this occasion, that these great thoroughfares dedicated to trade have closed their doors and covered up the insignias of commerce; that your great exchanges have closed and your citizens given themselves up to the observance of the celebration in which we are participating.

I believe that patriotism has been intensified in many hearts by what we have witnessed to-day. I believe that patriotism has been placed in a higher and holier fame in many hearts. The bunting with which you have covered your walls, these patriotic inscriptions, must go down and the wage and trade be resumed again. Here may I not ask you to carry those inscriptions that now hang on the walls into your homes, into the schools of your city, into all of your great institutions where children are gathered, and teach them that the eye of the young and the old should look upon that flag as one of the familiar glories of every American? Have we not learned that no stocks and bonds, nor land, is our country? It is a spiritual thought that is in our minds—it is the flag and what it stands for; it is the fireside and the home; it is the thoughts that are in our hearts, born of the inspiration which comes with the story of the flag, or martyrs to liberty. It is a graveyard into which a common country has gathered the unconscious deeds of those who died that the thing might live which we love and call our country, rather than anything that can be touched or seen.

Let me add a thought due to our country's future. Perhaps never have we been so well equipped for war upon land as now, and we have never seen the time when our people were more smitten with the love of peace. To elevate the morals of our people; to hold up the law as that sacred thing which, like the ark of God of old, may not be touched by irreverent hands, but frowns upon any attempt to dethrone its supremacy; to unite our people in all that makes home comfortable, as well as to give our energies in the direction of material advancement, this service may we render. And out of this great demonstration let us draw lessons to inspire us to consecrate ourselves anew to this love and service of our country.

HARRISON ON THE JOHNSTOWN FLOOD
June 4, 1889

On May 31, 1889, in rain-swept western Pennsylvania
swirling waters from a broken reservoir near Johnstown
took several thousand lives and ten million dollars
worth of property. At Willard's Hotel, hastily made a
relief depot, Harrison publicly urged that all help the
distressed. He led the way in subscribing personal
funds.

My fellow-citizens: Everyone here to-day is distressingly conscious of
the circumstances which have convened this meeting. It would be
wholly superfluous for me to attempt to set before you more impressively
than the newspapers have already done the horrors attending the calam-
ity which has fallen upon the city of Johnstown and the neighboring
hamlets in a large section of Pennsylvania situated on the Susquehanna
River. The grim pencil of Doré would be inadequate to portray the
distress and horrors of this visitation. In such meetings as we have
to-day here in the national capital, and other like gatherings that are
taking place in all the cities of this land, we have the only relief to
the distress and darkness of the picture. When such calamitous visita-
tions fall upon any section of our country we can only put about the
dark picture the golden border of love and charity. It is in such fires as
this that the brotherhood of men is welded. And where more appropri-
ately than here at the national capital can we give expression to that
sympathy and brotherhood which is now so strongly appealed to by the
distress of large bodies of our fellow-citizens?

I am glad to say that early this morning, from a city not long ago
visited with pestilence, and not long ago appealing to the charity of
the philanthropic people of the whole land for relief—the city of Jack-
sonville, Fla.—there came the reflex, the ebb of that tide of charity
which flowed toward them, in a telegram from the chairman of the
relief association of that city authorizing me to draw upon them for
$2,000 for the relief of the sufferers at Johnstown.

But this is no time for speech. While I talk men and women and
children are suffering for the relief which we plan to give to-day.

A word or two of practical suggestion and I will place this meeting
in the hands of those who have assembled here to give effect to our
loving purposes. I have to-day had a dispatch from the governor of
Pennsylvania advising me that communication has just been opened
with Williamsport, on a branch of the Susquehanna River, and that the

losses in that section have been appalling; that thousands of people there are hungry and homeless and penniless, and there is immediate urgency for food to relieve their necessities, and he advises me that any supplies of food that can be hastily gathered here should be sent direct to Williamsport, where they will be distributed. I suggest, therefore — and the occasion is such that bells might be rung in your streets to call the attention of the thoughtless to this great exigency — that a committee should be appointed to speedily collect contributions of food in order that a train loaded with provisions might be dispatched to-night or in the early morning to these sufferers.

I suggest, secondly, that as many of these people have had the entire furniture of their houses swept away, and have now only a temporary shelter, that a committee be appointed to collect from your citizens such articles of clothing, especially bedclothing, as can be spared; and, now that the summer season is on, there can hardly be many households in Washington that can not spare a blanket or a cover-lid for the relief of the suffering ones.

I suggest, thirdly, that, of your substantial business people, bankers, and others, there be appointed a committee, who shall collect money; for, after the first exigency has passed, there will be found in those communities very many who have lost their all, who will need aid in the reconstruction of their demolished homes and in furnishing them in order that they may be again inhabited.

Need I say, in conclusion, that as a temporary citizen of Washington it would give me great satisfaction if the national capital should so generously respond to this call of our distressed fellow-citizens as to be conspicuous among the cities of the land for its ample and generous answer.

I feel, as I am calling for subscriptions, that I should say that on Saturday, on being first apprised of the need at Johnstown, I telegraphed to the mayor of that city my subscription. I do not care now or at any time to speak of anything that is so personal as this, but I felt it due to you, as I am placed here to-day to solicit and urge others to give, that I should say so much as that.

PAN-AMERICAN CONFERENCE
October 2, 1889 to April 19, 1890

October 2, 1889 was chosen as the opening day for the Congress that envisioned a new inter-American system to be based on improved trade, diplomacy and mutual defense. Both Harrison and Secretary of State Blaine were committed to new directions in U.S.-Latin American relations. At the White House the International Congress opened. Blaine outlined the agenda that included a six weeks' tour of some 6,000 miles through northern and midwestern industrial centers by visiting delegates. Between November 18 and adjournment on April 19, 1890, the Congress met 70 times. A new Monroe Doctrine was in the making. On April 19 in the Executive Mansion Harrison bade the delegates farewell:

Gentlemen: I find in this parting call of the delegates of the Conference of American States both pain and pleasure. I participate in the regret which the delegates from the United States feel who are to part with those from other countries. I take pleasure in the knowledge of the fact that your labors have been brought to a happy conclusion. The differences of opinion have been happily reconciled. I remark with pleasure the proposition which will be productive of peace among the American States represented in the conference. It will be without excuse if one of them shall lift a hostile hand against the other. We gave you the other day a review of the small detachment of the American army—not to show you that we have an army, but that we have none; that our securities are lodged with our people and that they are safe.

We rejoice that you have found in the organization of our country something which commends itself to your own. We shall be glad to receive new lessons in return. In conclusion, I find much to approve in the frinedly purposes of the Conference toward this Government, and I bid each and every one of you a heartfelt good-bye.

In a series of special messages to Congress Harrison indicated some of the progress resulting from the Pan-American Conference.

AN INTERNATIONAL RAILWAY LINE

To the Senate and House of Representatives:

I transmit herewith a report of the International American Conference, recently in session at this capital, recommending a survey of a route for an intercontinental line of railroad to connect the systems of North America with those of the Southern Continent, and to be conducted under the direction of a board of commissioners representing the several American Republics.

Public attention has chiefly been attracted to the subject of improved water communication between the ports of the United States and those of Central and South America. The creation of new and improved steamship lines undoubtedly furnishes the readiest means of developing an increased trade with the Latin-American nations. But it should not be forgotten that it is possible to travel by land from Washington to the southernmost capital of South America, and that the opening of railroad communication with these friendly states will give to them and to us facilities for intercourse and the exchanges of trade that are of special value. The work contemplated is vast, but entirely practicable. It will be interesting to all and perhaps surprising to most of us to notice how much has already been done in the way of railroad construction in Mexico and South America that can be utilized as part of an intercontinental line. I do not hesitate to recommend that Congress make the very moderate appropriation for surveys suggested by the conference, and authorize the appointment of commissioners and the detail of engineer officers to direct and conduct the necessary preliminary surveys.

BENJAMIN HARRISON

EXECUTIVE MANSION
May 19, 1890

AN INTERNATIONAL AMERICAN BANK

To the Senate and House of Representatives:

I transmit herewith a letter from the Secretary of State, inclosing a report adopted by the International American Conference, recently in session at this capital, recommending the establishment of an international American bank, with its principal offices in the city of New York and branches in the commercial centers of the several other American Republics.

The advantages of such an institution to the merchants of the United States engaged in trade with Central and South America and the purposes intended to be accomplished are fully set forth in the letter of the Secretary of State and the accompanying report. It is not proposed to involve the United States in any financial responsibility, but only to give to the proposed bank a corporate franchise and to promote public confidence by requiring that its condition and transactions shall be submitted to a scrutiny similar to that which is now exercised over our domestic banking system.

The subject is submitted for the consideration of Congress in the belief that it will be found possible to promote the end desired by legislation so guarded as to avoid all just criticism.

BENJAMIN HARRISON

EXECUTIVE MANSION
May 27, 1890

THE INTERNATIONAL AMERICAN CONFERENCE

To the Senate and House of Representatives:

The International American Conference, recently in session at this capital, recommended for adoption by the several American Republics:

(1) A uniform system of customs regulations for the classification and valuation of imported merchandise;

(2) A uniform nomenclature for the description of articles of merchandise imported and exported; and

(3) The establishment at Washington of an international bureau of information.

The conference also, at its final session, decided to establish in the city of Washington, as a fitting memorial of its meeting, a Latin-American library, to be formed by contributions from the several nations of historical, geographical, and literary works, maps, manuscripts, and official documents relating to the history and civilization of America, and expressed a desire that the Government of the United States should provide a suitable building for the shelter of such a library, to be solemnly dedicated upon the four-hundredth anniversary of the discovery of America.

The importance of these suggestions is fully set forth in the letter of the Secretary of State, and the accompanying documents herewith transmitted, to which I invite your attention.

BENJAMIN HARRISON

EXECUTIVE MANSION
June 2, 1890

RECIPROCAL COMMERCIAL TREATIES

To the Senate and House of Representatives:

I transmit herewith, for your information, a letter from the Secretary of State, inclosing a report of the International American Conference, which recommends that reciprocal commercial treaties be entered into between the United States and the several other Republics of this hemisphere.

It has been so often and so persistently stated that our tariff laws offered an insurmountable barrier to a large exchange of products with the Latin-American nations, that I deem it proper to call especial attention to the fact that more than 87 percent of the products of those nations sent to our ports are now admitted free. If sugar is placed upon the free list, practically every important article exported from those States will be given untaxed access to our markets, except wool. The real difficulty in the way of negotiating profitable reciprocity treaties is, that we have given freely so much that would have had value in the mutual concessions which such treaties imply. I can not doubt, however, that the present advantages which the products of these near and friendly States enjoy in our markets—though they are not by law exclusive—will, with other considerations, favorably dispose them to adopt such measures, by treaty or otherwise, as will tend to equalize and greatly enlarge our mutual exchanges.

It will certainly be time enough for us to consider whether we must cheapen the cost of production by cheapening labor, in order to gain access to the South American markets, when we have fairly tried the effect of established and reliable steam communication, and of convenient methods of money exchanges. There can be no doubt, I think, that with these facilities well established, and with a rebate of duties upon imported raw materials used in the manufacture of goods for export, our merchants will be able to compete in the ports of the Latin-American nations with those of any other country.

If after the Congress shall have acted upon pending tariff legislation it shall appear that, under the general treaty-making power, or under any special powers given by law, our trade with the States represented in the Conference can be enlarged upon a basis of mutual advantage, it will be promptly done.

BENJAMIN HARRISON

EXECUTIVE MANSION
June 19, 1890

POSTAL AND CABLE COMMUNICATION
WITH SOUTH AMERICA

To the Senate and House of Representatives:

I transmit herewith a letter from the Secretary of State, inclosing the recommendations of the International American Conference for the establishment of improved facilities for postal and cable communication between the United States and the several countries of Central and South America.

I can not too strongly urge upon Congress the necessity of giving this subject immediate and favorable consideration, and of making adequate appropriations to carry the recommendations into effect; and in this connection I beg leave to call attention to what was said on the subject in my annual message. The delegates of the seventeen neighboring republics which have so recently been assembled in Washington, at the invitation of this Government, have expressed their wish and purpose to cooperate with the United States in the adoption of measures to improve the means of communication between the several republics of America. They recognize the necessity of frequent, regular, and rapid steamship service, both for the purpose of maintaining friendly intercourse and for the convenience of commerce, and realize that without such facilities it is useless to attempt to extend the trade between their ports and ours.

BENJAMIN HARRISON

EXECUTIVE MANSION
July 2, 1890

THE SHERMAN ANTI-TRUST ACT
July 2, 1890

The growth of trusts and corporations, coupled with some malpractices of big business, led to a growing demand for the regulation of trusts by the Federal Government. In his Inaugural Harrison repeated his pledge to secure such anti-trust legislation. The final bill, which bears Sherman's name, was chiefly drawn by Harrison's cronies, Senators Hoar and Edmunds. Its importance rests with the fact that it was the first federal act which attempted to regulate trusts. It suffered from ambiguous language that failed to define trust, restraint, monopoly, and it was unclear whether its terms included labor as well as capital.

An Act to protect trade and commerce against unlawful restraints and monopolies. . . .

Be it enacted

SEC. 1. Every contract, combination in the form of trust or otherwise, or conspiracy, in restraint of trade or commerce among the several States, or with foreign nations, is hereby declared to be illegal. Every person who shall make any such contract or engage in any such combination or conspiracy, shall be deemed guilty of a misdemeanor, and, on conviction thereof, shall be punished by fine not exceeding five thousand dollars, or by imprisonment not exceeding one year, or by both said punishments, in the discretion of the court.

SEC. 2. Every person who shall monopolize, or attempt to monopolize, or combine or conspire with any other person or persons, to monopolize any part of the trade or commerce among the several States, or with foreign nations, shall be deemed guilty of a misdemeanor, and, on conviction thereof, shall be punished by fine not exceeding five thousand dollars, or by imprisonment not exceeding one year, or by both said punishments, in the discretion of the court.

SEC. 3. Every contract, combination in form of trust or otherwise, or conspiracy, in restraint of trade or commerce in any Territory of the United States or of the District of Columbia, or in restraint of trade or commerce between any such Territory and another, or between any such Territory or Territories and any State or States or the District of Columbia, or with foreign nations, or between the District of Columbia and any State or States or foreign nations, is hereby declared illegal. Every person who shall make any such contract or engage in any such combination or conspiracy, shall be deemed guilty of a misdemeanor, and, on conviction thereof, shall be punished by fine not exceeding five thousand dollars, or by imprisonment not exceeding one year, or by both said punishments, in the discretion of the court.

SEC. 4. The several circuit courts of the United States are hereby invested with jurisdiction to prevent and restrain violations of this act; and it shall be the duty of the several district attorneys of the United States, in their respective districts, under the direction of the Attorney-General, to institute proceedings in equity to prevent and restrain such violations. Such proceedings may be by way of petition setting forth the case and praying that such violation shall be enjoined or otherwise prohibited. When the parties complained of shall have been duly notified of such petition the courts shall proceed, as soon as may be, to the hearing and determination of the case; and pending such petition and before final decrees, the court may at any time make such temporary restraining order or prohibition as shall be deemed just in the premises.

SEC. 5. Whenever it shall appear to the court before which any proceeding under Section four of this act may be pending, that the ends of justice require that other parties should be brought before the court, the court may cause them to be summoned, whether they reside in the district in which the court is held or not; and subpoenas to that end may be served in any district by the marshal thereof.

SEC. 6. Any property owned under any contract or by any combination, or pursuant to any conspiracy (and being the subject thereof) mentioned in Section one of this act, and being in the course of transportation from one State to another, or to a foreign country, shall be forfeited to the United States, and may be seized and condemned by like proceedings as those provided by law for the forfeiture, seizure, and condemnation of property imported into the United States contrary to law.

SEC. 7. Any person who shall be injured in his business or property by any other person or corporation by reason of anything forbidden or declared to be unlawful by this act, may sue therefor in any circuit court of the United States in the district in which the defendant resides or is found, without respect to the amount in controversy, and shall recover threefold the damages by him sustained, and the costs of suit, including a reasonable attorney's fee.

SEC. 8. That the word "person," or "persons," wherever used in this act shall be deemed to include corporations and associations existing under or authorized by the laws of either the United States, the laws of any of the Territories, the laws of any State, or the laws of any foreign country.

THE SHERMAN SILVER PURCHASE ACT
July 14, 1890

The Bland-Allison Act of 1878 had satisfied neither silver nor gold advocates. The 1890 law represented a new compromise engineered by Harrison. On the whole it seemed to favor the silver elements. The concessions made to silver were in return for western support of the McKinley tariff of 1890.

An Act directing the purchase of silver bullion and the issue of Treasury notes thereon, and for other purposes.

Be it enacted . . ., That the Secretary of the Treasury is hereby directed to purchase, from time to time, silver bullion to the aggregate amount of four million five hundred thousand ounces, or so much thereof as may be offered in each month, at the market price thereof, not exceeding one dollar for three hundred and seventy-one and twenty-five hundredths grains of pure silver, and to issue in payment for such purchases of silver bullion Treasury notes of the United States to be prepared by the Secretary of the Treasury, in such form and of such denominations, not less than one dollar nor more than one thousand dollars, as he may prescribe. . . .

SEC. 2. That the Treasury notes issued in accordance with the provisions of this act shall be redeemable on demand, in coin, at the Treasury of the United States, or at the office of any assistant treasurer of the United States, and when so redeemed may be reissued; but no greater or less amount of such notes shall be outstanding at any time than the cost of the silver bullion and the standard silver dollars coined therefrom, then held in the Treasury purchased by such notes; and such Treasury notes shall be a legal tender in payment of all debts, public and private, except where otherwise expressly stipulated in the contract, and shall be receivable for customs, taxes, and all public dues, and when so received may be reissued; and such notes, when held by any national banking association, may be counted as a part of its lawful reserve. That upon demand of the holder of any of the Treasury notes herein provided for the Secretary of the Treasury shall, under such regulations as he may prescribe, redeem such notes in gold or silver coin, at his discretion, it being the established policy of the United States to maintain the two metals on a parity with each other upon the present legal ratio, or such ratio as may be provided by law.

SEC. 3. That the Secretary of the Treasury shall each month coin two million ounces of the silver bullion purchased under the provisions of this act into standard dollars until July 1, 1891, and after that time he shall coin of the silver bullion purchased under the provisions of this act as much as may be necessary to provide for the redemption of the Treasury notes herein provided for, and any gain or seigniorage arising from such coinage shall be accounted for and paid into the Treasury. . . .

THE LOUISIANA STATE LOTTERY
July 29, 1890

The Louisiana lottery spread a morass of corruption across the country as well as within the Bayou State. Household funds, grocery money and office cash were spent in search of phantom gold. In his first message to Congress Harrison had asked for a more stringent law to deny U.S. mails to lottery promoters. When the finger of corruption and bribery touched Washington, D.C. and the infant state of North Dakota, Harrison called for a full investigation and repeated a warning to Congress with the special message produced below. He secured prompt action in both House and Senate. On September 19, 1890, he signed the anti-lottery bill into law.

To the Senate and House of Representatives:

The recent attempt to secure a charter from the State of North Dakota for a lottery company, the pending effort to obtain from the State of Louisiana a renewal of the charter of the Louisiana State Lottery, and the establishment of one or more lottery companies at Mexican towns near our border, have served the good purpose of calling public attention to an evil of vast proportions. If the baneful effects of the lotteries were confined to the States that give the companies corporate powers and a license to conduct the business, the citizens of other States, being powerless to apply legal remedies, might clear themselves of responsibility by the use of such moral agencies as were within their reach. But the case is not so. The people of all the States are debauched and defrauded. The vast sums of money offered to the States for charters are drawn from the people of the United States, and the General Government, through its mail system, is made the effective and profitable medium of intercourse between the lottery company and its victims. The use of the mails is quite as essential to the companies as the State license. It would be practically impossible for these companies to exist if the public mails were once effectively closed against their advertisements and remittances. The use of the mails by these companies is a prostitution of an agency only intended to serve the purposes of legitimate trade and a decent social intercourse.

It is not necessary, I am sure, for me to attempt to portray the robbery of the poor and the wide-spread corruption of public and private morals which are the necessary incidents of these lottery schemes.

The national capital has become a sub-headquarters of the Louisiana Lottery Company, and its numerous agents and attorneys are conducting here a business involving probably a larger use of the mails than that of any legitimate business enterprise in the District of Columbia. There seems to be good reason to believe that the corrupting touch of these agents has been felt by the clerks in the postal service and by some of the police officers of the District.

Severe and effective legislation should be promptly enacted to enable the Post-Office Department to purge the mails of all letters, newspapers, and circulars relating to the business.

The letter of the Postmaster-General, which I transmit herewith, points out the inadequacy of the existing statutes, and suggests legislation that would be effective.

It may also be necessary to so regulate the carrying of letters by the express companies as to prevent the use of those agencies to maintain communication between the lottery companies and their agents or customers in other States.

It does not seem possible that there can be any division of sentiment as to the propriety of closing the mails against these companies, and I therefore venture to express the hope that such proper powers as are necessary to that end will be at once given to the Post-Office Department.

BENJAMIN HARRISON

EXECUTIVE MANSION
July 29, 1890

G.A.R. NATIONAL ENCAMPMENT
Boston, Mass., August 12, 1890

At the height of the congressional debate over the McKinley tariff bill, Harrison sailed to Boston to address his Grand Army of the Republic comrades. He spoke several times and Congressman William McKinley and Henry Cabot Lodge reviewed a spectacular parade from Harrison's box. The presidential address reveals his facility of phrase in remarking upon patriotism and love of country.

Mr. Chairman and Comrades of the Grand Army of the Republic: I had impressions both pleasurable and painful as I looked upon the great procession of veterans which swept through the streets of this historic capital to-day; pleasurable in the contemplation of so many faces of those who shared together the perils and glories of the great struggle for the Union; sensations of a mournful sort as I thought how seldom we should meet again. Not many times more here. As I have stood in the great National Cemetery at Arlington and have seen those silent battalions of the dead, I have thought how swiftly the reaper is doing his work and how soon in the scattered cemeteries of the land the ashes of all the soldiers of the great war shall be gathered to honored graves. And yet I could not help but feel that in the sturdy tread of those battalions there was yet strength of heart and limb that would not be withheld if a present peril should confront the Nation that you love. And if Arlington is the death, we see to-day in the springing step of those magnificent battalions of the Sons of Veterans the resurrection. They are coming on to take our places; the Nation will not be defenseless when we are gone, but those who have read about the firesides of the veterans' homes, in which they have been born and reared, the lessons of patriotism and the stories of heroism will come fresh armed to any conflict that may confront us in the future.

And so to-night we may gather from this magnificent spectacle a fresh and strong sense of security for the permanency of our country and our free institutions. I thought it altogether proper that I should take a brief furlough from official duties at Washington to mingle with you here to-day as a comrade, because every President of the United States must realize that the strength of the Government, its defense in war, the army that is to muster under its banner when our nation is assailed, is to be found here in the masses of our people. And so, as my furlough is almost done, and the train is already waiting that must bear me back to Washington, I can only express again the cordial, sincere, and fraternal interest which I feel this day in meeting you all. I can only hope that God will so order the years that are left to you that for you and those who are dear to you they may be ordered in all gentleness and sweetness, in all prosperity and success, and that, when at last the comrades who survive you shall wrap the flag of the Union about your body and bear it to the grave, you may die in peace and in the hope of a glorious resurrection.

Grave diplomatic problems arising from capital crimes occupied the President and the State Department for many months in 1891 and 1892. Two ugly episodes were largely concurrent, and for a time war was threatened on both sides of the globe. The two nations concerned were Italy and Chile.
The Mafia Incident occurred in mid-October, 1890. New Orleans Police Chief was allegedly murdered by members of the Mafia. The report threatened New Orleans with a bloody riot, with white Americans threatening to lynch those Italian immigrants charged with murdering a law-enforcement officer.

ANNUAL MESSAGE TO CONGRESS
December 1, 1890

Harrison stated that "no community will find lawlessness profitable," adding: "No community can afford to have it known that the officers who are charged with the preservation of the public peace and the restraint of criminal classes are themselves the product of fraud or violence. The magistrate is then without respect, the law without sanction." On March 14, 1891, however, some citizens in New Orleans took the law into their own hands and lynched eleven Italians charged with the murder of the police chief six months earlier. A nearly complete diplomatic break with Italy was followed by talk of war.

ANNUAL MESSAGE TO CONGRESS
December 9, 1891

. . . The lynching at New Orleans in March last of eleven men of Italian nativity by a mob of citizens was a most deplorable and discreditable incident. It did not, however, have its origin in any general animosity to the Italian people, nor in any disrespect to the Government of Italy, with which our relations were of the most friendly character. The fury of the mob was directed against these men as the supposed participants or accessories in the murder of a city officer. I do not allude to this as mitigating in any degree this offense against law and humanity, but only as affecting the international questions which grew out of it. It was at once represented by the Italian minister that several of those whose lives had been taken by the mob were Italian subjects, and a demand was made for the punishment of the participants and for an indemnity to the families of those who were killed. It is to be regretted that the manner in which these claims were presented was not such as to promote a calm discussion of the questions involved; but this may well be attributed to the excitement and indignation which the crime naturally evoked. The views of this Government as to its obligations to foreigners domiciled here were fully stated in the correspondence, as well as its purpose to make an investigation of the affair with a view to determine whether there were present any circumstances that could, under such rules of duty as we had indicated, create an obligation upon the United States. The temporary absence of a minister plenipotentiary of Italy at this capital has retarded the further correspondence, but it is not doubted that a friendly conclusion is attainable.

Some suggestions growing out of this unhappy incident are worthy of the attention of Congress. It would, I believe, be entirely competent for Congress to make offenses against the treaty rights of foreigners domiciled in the United States cognizable in the Federal courts. This has not, however, been done, and the Federal officers and courts have no power in such cases to intervene either for the protection of a foreign citizen or for the punishment of his slayers. It seems to me to follow, in this state of the law, that the officers of the State charged with police and judicial powers in such cases must, in the consideration of international questions growing out of such incidents, be regarded in such sense as Federal agents as to make this Government answerable for their acts in cases where it would be answerable if the United States had used its constitutional power to define and punish crimes against treaty rights. . . .

STRAINED RELATIONS WITH CHILE

Also in his annual message to Congress in 1891
President Harrison set down the events that followed
civil war in Chile.

The civil war in Chile, which began in January last, was continued, but fortunately with infrequent and not important armed collisions, until August 28, when the Congressional forces landed near Valparaiso and, after a bloody engagement, captured that city. President Balmaceda at once recognized that his cause was lost, and a provisional government was speedily established by the victorious party. Our minister was promptly directed to recognize and put himself in communication with this Government so soon as it should have established its *de facto* character, which was done. During the pendency of the civil contest frequent indirect appeals were made to this Government to extend belligerent rights to the insurgents and to give audience to their representatives. This was declined, and that policy was pursued throughout which this Government, when wrenched by civil war, so strenuously insisted upon on the part of European nations. The *Itata*, an armed vessel commanded by a naval officer of the insurgent fleet, manned by its sailors and with soldiers on board, was seized under process of the United States court at San Diego, California, for a violation of our neutrality laws. While in the custody of an officer of the court the vessel was forcibly wrested from his control and put to sea. It would have been inconsistent with the dignity and self-respect of this Government not to have insisted that the *Itata* should be returned to San Diego to abide the judgment of the court. This was so clear to the Junta of the Congressional party, established at Iquique, that before the arrival of the *Itata* at that port the secretary of foreign relations of the provisional government addressed to Rear-Admiral Brown, commanding the United States naval forces, a communication, from which the following is an extract:

"The Provisional Government has learned by the cablegrams of the Associated Press that the transport *Itata*, detained in San Diego by order of the United States for taking on board munitions of war and in possession of the marshal, left the port, carrying on board this official, who was landed at a point near the coast, and then continued her voyage. . . . If this news be correct. this Government would deplore the conduct of the *Itata*, and as an evidence that it is not disposed to support or agree to the infraction of the laws of the United States, the undersigned takes advantage of the personal relations you have been good enough to maintain with him since your arrival in this port to declare to you that as soon as she is within reach of our orders this Government will put the *Itata*, with the arms and munitions she took on board in San Diego, at the disposition of the United States."

A trial in the district court of the United States for the southern district of California has recently resulted in a decision holding, among other things, that, inasmuch as the Congressional party had not been recognized as a belligerent, the acts done in its interest could not be a violation of our neutrality laws. From this judgment the United States has appealed, not that the condemnation of the vessel is a matter of importance, but that we may know what the present state of our law is; for, if this construction of the statute is correct, there is obvious necessity for revision and amendment.

During the progress of the war in Chile this Government tendered its good offices to bring about a peaceful adjustment, and it was at one time hoped that a good result might be reached; but in this we were disappointed.

The instructions to our naval officers and to our minister at Santiago, from the first to the last of this struggle enjoined upon them the most impartial treatment and absolute noninterference. I am satisfied that these instructions were observed and that our representatives were always watchful to use their influence impartially in the interest of humanity, and, on more than one occasion, did so effectively. We could not forget, however, that this Government was in diplomatic relations with the then established Government of Chile, as it is now in such relations with the successor of that Government. I am quite sure that President Montt, who has under circumstances of promise for the peace of Chile, been installed as President of that Republic, will not desire that, in the unfortunate event of any revolt against his authority, the policy of this Government should be other than that which we have recently observed. No official complaint of the conduct of our minister or of our naval officers during the struggle has been presented to this Government; and it is a matter of regret that so many of our own people should have given ear to unofficial charges and complaints that manifestly had their origin in rival interests and in a wish to pervert the relations of the United States with Chile.

The collapse of the government of Balmaceda brought about a condition which is unfortunately too familiar in the history of the Central and South American states. With the overthrow of the Balmaceda government, he and many of his councilors and officers became at once fugitives for their lives and appealed to the commanding officers of the foreign naval vessels in the harbor of Valparaiso and to the resident foreign ministers at Santiago for asylum. This asylum was freely given, according to my information, by the naval vessels of several foreign powers and by several of the legations at Santiago. The American minister, as well as his colleagues, acting upon the impulses of humanity, extended asylum to political refugees whose lives were in peril. I have not been willing to direct the surrender of such of these persons as are still in the American legation without suitable conditions.

It is believed that the Government of Chile is not in a position, in view of the precedents with which it has been connected, to broadly deny the right of asylum, and the correspondence has not thus far presented any such denial. The treatment of our minister for a time was such as to call for a decided protest, and it was very gratifying to observe that unfriendly measures, which were undoubtedly the result of the prevailing excitement, were at once rescinded or suitably relaxed.

On the 16th of October an event occurred in Valparaiso so serious and tragic in its circumstances and results as to very justly excite the indignation of our people and to call for prompt and decided action on the part of this Government. A considerable number of the sailors of the U.S.S. *Baltimore*, then in the harbor of Valparaiso, being upon shore-leave and unarmed, were assaulted by armed men nearly simultaneously in different localities in the city. One petty officer was killed outright and seven or eight seamen were seriously wounded, one of whom has since died. So savage and brutal was the assault that several of our sailors received more than two, and one as many as eighteen, stab wounds. An investigation of the affair was promptly made by a board of officers of the *Baltimore*, and their report shows that these assaults were unprovoked, that our men were conducting themselves in a peaceable and orderly manner, and that some of the police of the city took part in the assault and used their weapons with fatal effect, while a few others, with some well-disposed citizens, endeavored to protect our men. Thirty-six of our sailors were arrested, and some of them, while being taken to prison, were cruelly beaten and maltreated. The fact that they were all discharged, no criminal charge being lodged against any one of them, shows very clearly that they were innocent of any breach of peace.

So far as I have yet been able to learn no other explanation of this bloody work has been suggested than that it had its origin in hostility to these men as sailors of the United States, wearing the uniform of their Government, and not in any individual act of personal animosity. The attention of the Chilean Government was at once called to this affair, and a statement of the facts obtained by the investigation we had conducted was submitted, accompanied by a request to be advised of any other or qualifying facts in the possession of the Chilean Government that might tend to relieve this affair of the appearance of an insult to this Government. The Chilean Government was also advised that if such qualifying facts did not exist this Government would confidently expect full and prompt reparation.

It is to be regretted that the reply of the secretary for foreign affairs of the Provisional Government was couched in an offensive tone. To this no response has been made. This Government is now awaiting the result of an investigation which has been conducted by the criminal court at Valparaiso. It is reported unofficially that the investigation is about completed, and it is expected that the result will soon be communicated to this Government, together with some adequate and satisfactory response to the note by which the attention of Chile was called to this incident. If these just expectations should be disappointed or further needless delay intervene, I will, by a special message, bring this matter again to the attention of Congress for such action as may be necessary.

> *Chile then publicly attacked and maligned Harrison. War clouds thickened. U.S. sent an ultimatum to Chile and on January 25, 1892, Harrison sent a long special message to Congress, requesting "such action as may be deemed appropriate." Chile capitulated and on January 28, 1892, Harrison sent a second special message to Congress:*

I transmit herewith additional correspondence between this Government and the Government of Chile, consisting of a note of Mr. Montt, the Chilean minister at this capital to Mr. Blaine, dated January 23; a reply of Mr. Blaine thereto of date January 27; and a dispatch from Mr. Egan, our minister at Santiago, transmitting the response of Mr. Pereira, the Chilean minister of foreign affairs to the note of Mr. Blaine of January 21, which was received by me on the 26th instant. The note of Mr. Montt to Mr. Blaine, though dated January 23, was not delivered at the State Department until after 12 o'clock, meridian, of the 25th, and was not translated and its receipt notified to me until late in the afternoon of that day.

The response of Mr. Pereira to our note of the 21st withdraws, with acceptable expressions of regret, the offensive note of Mr. Matta of the 11th ultimo, and also the request for the recall of Mr. Egan. The treatment of the incident of the assault upon the sailors of the *Baltimore* is so conciliatory and friendly that I am of the opinion that there is a good prospect that the differences growing out of that serious affair can now be adjusted upon terms satisfactory to this Government, by the usual methods and without special powers from Congress. This turn in the affair is very gratifying to me, as I am sure it will be to Congress and to our people. The general support of the efforts of the Executive to enforce the just rights of the nation in this matter has given an instructive and useful illustration of the unity and patriotism of our people. Should it be necessary, I will again communicate with Congress upon the subject.

THE ANNEXATION OF HAWAII
Harrison's Message Transmitting Treaty of Annexation
February 13, 1893

In the Hawaiian Islands, long of interest to Harrison and his Cabinet, a revolution unseated the native Queen. A Provisional President and colleagues drew up a treaty of annexation and sent a commission to Washington to ask acceptance. Harrison viewed annexation as a fitting climax to his expansive foreign policy but regretted that the request had not come six months earlier.

EXECUTIVE MANSION
Washington, February 15, 1893

To the Senate:

I transmit herewith, with a view to its ratification, a treaty of annexation concluded on the 14th day of February, 1893, between John W. Foster, Secretary of Sate, . . . and Lorin A. Thurston, W.R. Castle, W.C. Wilder, C.L. Carter, and Joseph Marsden, the commissioners on the part of the Government of the Hawaiian Islands.

I do not deem it necessary to discuss at any length the conditions which have resulted in this decisive action. It has been the policy of the Administration not only to respect but to encourage the continuance of an independent government in the Hawaiian Islands so long as it afforded suitable guaranties for the protection of life and property and maintained a stability and strength that gave adequate security against the domination of any other power. The moral support of this Government has continually manifested itself in the most friendly diplomatic relations and in many acts of courtesy to the Hawaiian rulers.

The overthrow of the monarchy was not in any way promoted by this Government, but had its origin in what seems to have been a reactionary and revolutionary policy on the part of Queen Liliuokalani, which put in serious peril not only the large and preponderating interests of the United States in the islands, but all foreign interests, and, indeed, the decent administration of civil affairs and the peace of the islands. It is quite evident that the monarchy had become effete and the Queen's Government so weak and inadequate as to be the prey of designing and unscrupulous persons. The restoration of Queen Liliuokalani to her throne is undesirable, if not impossible, and unless actively supported by the United States would be accompanied by serious disaster and the disorganization of all business interests. The influence and interest of the United States in the islands must be increased and not diminished. Only two courses are now open—one the establishment of a protectorate by the United States, and the other annexation full and complete. I think the latter course, which has been adopted in the treaty, will be highly promotive of the best interests of the Hawaiian people, and is the only one that will adequately secure the interests of the United States. These interests are not wholly selfless. It is essential that none of the other great powers shall secure these islands. Such a possession would not consist with our safety and with the peace of the world. This view of the situation is so apparent and conclusive that no protest has been heard from any government against proceedings looking to annexation. Every foreign representative at Honolulu promptly acknowledged the Provisional Government, and I think there is a general concurrence in the opinion that the deposed Queen ought not to be restored.

Prompt action upon this treaty is very desirable. . . .

HARRISON ON THE SPANISH-AMERICAN WAR
Asbury Park, N.J., July 4, 1898
Long Branch, N.J., July 5, 1898

At the height of the war with Spain Harrison was vacationing along the Jersey shore. On two successive days he spoke on the progress of the war, thus revealing publicly his thoughts on the morality of American involvement. The first address was made as guest of honor at the banquet of the Society of the Cincinnati, held at the Hathaway Inn, Asbury Park, N.J.

I recall with pride that this great natal day of our independence is made memorable by the fall of Vicksburg and now again by the capture of the first Spanish stronghold in Cuba. I am one of those who did not see how war could be avoided. When is it possible for an American to see a woman beaten by a brute and not raise a punishing arm? When 200,000 men and women are permitted to starve by the callous cruelty of a barbarous nation, then I believe the power of that nation must be effaced from the islands they have so abused.

Our grievances in 1776 pale by the side of the barbarous cruelties practiced by Spain. Let the Germans and Frenchmen say what they will, this is no war of conquest, but a war for humanity. Europe feels as she never felt before for America. Dewey's first glorious achievement at Manila set the pace and has made it impossible that any vessel of our navy or any regiment of our army should ever falter in the face of the enemy.

It is time for Europe to understand that the American navy is the match for any navy in the world. The sneers over there are forced, and now we are glad to know that our land forces, who do not fight at 3,000 yards, but look into the very eye of the adversary, have shown around the hills of Santiago that they keep pace with the gallant navy.

In the West an impression prevails that our New York and Eastern millionaires are a dilly-dally, washy kind of a set. But we have seen the cowboy and the millionaire dash up the bloody slopes side by side. We have discovered that wealth does not necessarily enfeeble or sap the patriotism of the American heart. Then again we have witnessed the boys who wore the gray in 1861 fighting in the ranks with the boys who wore the blue. I have always felt that when Texas charged with Massachusetts and New Jersey the charge would be invincible.

And now we have another band of hero dead. These fallen soldiers ennoble a nation more than the achievements of commerce. Believe me, gentlemen, out of this war will come increased prosperity and a more united people, possessed of a mighty power that will insure protection and safety for all time to come.

IN BEHALF OF THE RED CROSS SOCIETY
Long Branch, N.J., July 5, 1898

We had heard, before the declaration of war, of the barbarities that were being perpetrated in Cuba. They seemed to pass belief. That quiet recital made by Senator Proctor, of Vermont, in the United States Senate, aroused the nation.

I do not think there has been made in any legislative assembly in the world in fifty years a speech that so powerfully affected the public sentiment as that. And yet there was not a lurid adjective in the speech. It was a restrained description of the barbarities practiced chiefly upon women and children by the Spanish rulers in Cuba. Senator Proctor said to me in conversation in New York: "I could not in the senate recite the worst of the atrocities of which I found evidence in Cuba. The treatment of the women among the reconcentrados was too brutal to be spoken of in public."

Could we stand by and not correct those who could be capable of perpetrating them? It seemed to me not. The cries of these starving women and children penetrated our bed chambers and came to us like ghastly visions of the night, and for one I could not understand why God made this nation great and strong if it was not for an hour and a work like that. We have said to the whole world this is the exclusive sphere of American influence, and by that declaration we proclaimed our duty to repress such atrocities as were being perpetrated in Cuba.

The war is waged on Red Cross lines, for humanity, for the relief and succor of the starving and the helpless. And how magnificently it has been waged! Can human sympathy be too large, can women's love be too strong for those brave fellows of our army and navy who have added new glory to the standard of the nation and have greatly lifted it in the respect of those countries of Europe that respect only war power?

The comfort of a sheeted bed and what your Western boys used to call a 'boiled shirt' is indescribable to those who have never missed the comforts of their homes, and when there is added the gentle ministration of women, a vision of the open door of heaven seems to come to fever-stricken, wounded men.

AMERICA HAS NO COMMISSION FROM GOD
TO POLICE THE WORLD
Paris, July 4, 1899

While in Paris as counsel for Venezuela during the summer of 1899, Harrison used Independence Day to speak on Franco-American relations, the Supreme Court, and on U.S. foreign policy as non-colonial. As early as May 3, 1898 he called the Spanish-American War "a war for humanity" but refused to say that "we have God's commission to deliver the oppressed the world around."

The observance of the anniversary of the American declaration of independence in France has a peculiar interest to me. We observe the great event—not in the land immediately affected by it, the dear homeland—but in the land of Lafayette, the land whose sympathetic interest and whose large trust in a poor and struggling people did so much to convert the declared right to be free into the fact of freedom. We may believe—but we can not affirm it—that in the longer end we alone might have won our freedom. In an extremity that seemed to make the result of our appeal to France determinative, she gave us succor—of money to replenish an exhausted treasury, of gallant men to fill our depleted ranks, of ships to break harassing blockades, and to protect our ravaged coasts. Mr. President, the patriotic sire has handed down to his patriotic sons this story of a generous intervention. It is not a forgotten episode—it is told every year in our public schools to hundreds of thousands of our American youth. We have grown strong, but we have not ceased to be grateful.

When America forgets her debt to France she will be unworthy and incapable of an international friendship. Mr. President, we have other friends, but we have none whose friendship involves or implies enmity to France. We are pleased when she is prosperous and grieved when she is troubled.

France has quite naturally adopted for herself the republican form of government which she helped us to establish—and we believe her people have given to their civil institutions their hearty and enduring allegiance. That, Mr. President, is in my opinion the test—a constitution, a form of government, a body of civil institutions, to which the love and allegiance of the people are given. Men may come and men may go, but the government endures. The course of events, the public thought may be influenced by great men, but the anchor holds—they may not supplant the constitution. The man on horseback, the man with a cockade, is not to be feared—the love of the people is set upon something that endures. This, Mr. President, is the security of the United States, and will be the security of every free people that cultivates it.

Our public men, our political parties, often divide upon questions affecting the construction of our written constitution; but with all our varying thoughts of what it is in this particular or in that, we give our allegiance to it, and not to our leaders. Fortunately for our peace, the American constitution provides a tribunal for the final and unappealable decision of all questions affecting the construction of the constitution, and, at the same time, opens a way by which it may be made to express the popular thought, but one not so easy as to give way to hasty and unconsidered popular feeling.

Washington spoke of the supreme court, as organized under our constitution, at one time as the keystone of our federal arch, and at another as the great pillar that bears up the fabric of our civil institutions. Its decisions have now and then evoked protests from the people, and these—in at least one instance—obtained that wide concurrence of the states which was necessary to make the constitution conform in that particular to the will of the people. But, speaking broadly, this great tribunal has even more than realized Washington's high conception of its value. A tribunal whose decision in all matters between individuals, or between individuals and the state, is accepted, if not with full assent, at least with loyal acquiescence, is essential to social and public tranquillity.

The United States is most favorably situated for the cultivation of peaceful relations with other nations. In the affairs of nations beyond seas, no question of the balance of power has ever disturbed us. Our neighbors could not contest our supremacy, but we will never use our power to their disadvantage.

If the thought of any general scheme of colonization could now enter the mind of any American statesman, it would surely be corrected by the manifest fact that the islands and the continents have already been divided. The United States is not, I am sure, ambitious to take the crumbs that remain. Her policy always has been, and I am sure we will not depart from it, to preserve the most friendly relations with all the nations of the world, and to extend her commerce, not by force of arms, but by the enticements and advantages of her superior products. She has never failed, whether in Greece, in Armenia, or in South America, to let it be known that she reprobated cruelty and persecution, but she has not felt that she had a commission to police the world.

She would gladly have welcomed the settlement of the Cuban question by the establishment of a humane, just and liberal government of that island under Spain. It was only because she believed that the true purposes of government, the ends for which it is constituted, had been lost sight of there, and because Cuba was almost in sight of her shores, and the cries of her people entered into her sleep, that she intervened. The American people will rejoice if the Cubans shall establish a free, stable, independent government. We have incurred responsibilities there and in the Philippines, and we will not fail to discharge them—at any cost.

It is too late to debate the question whether it might not have been wiser to have made our campaign in the Philippines purely a naval campaign, or the other question whether destiny or our own choice involved us there. We have assumed responsibilites toward the peaceable people there, toward Spain and toward the world, and we must establish order as a necessary preliminary to the consideration of any question as to the ultimate destiny or disposition of the archipelago.

We are proud of the achievements of our army and navy, and are glad if European misapprehension as to our naval construction and seamanship is removed. We are glad if a truer appreciation of the vast war resources of the United States prevails, glad only because it gives security in the hemisphere in which we are placed, not because it is a threat to Europe.

American diplomacy has been, I think, peculiarly sentimental. Our moral intervention for the oppressed and our later intervention by arms have been in the interest of liberty, not of gain.

It will not be thought unnatural, in spite of all past differences and strifes, if a peculiar friendliness should be felt by us for those of our language and race across the channel, but no one has suggested, Mr. President, that by reason of this natural and influential fact and motive, either Great Britain or the United States should assume all the animosities and quarrels of the other. The contingency of a general combination of all the powers against one or the other of these nations, threatening its destruction, need not be taken much account of until it arises. Suffice it to say that the friendship of the United States for Great Britain is not enmity to the world. A high sense of what is right and honorable, a due sense of obligation, fairness in our commercial intercourse, toward all who will allow us to be friendly, are, I think, the American thought and policy.

Mr. President, the United States now more than ever sympathizes with every practicable suggestion and movement that tends to diminish the influence of arms in the determination of international questions. Arbitration has halted because of the difficulty there has been in finding a purely judicial tribunal, one that would consider international questions with the same indifference to the parties and the same impartiality of judgment which characterizes our courts in the trial of questions between individuals. When such a tribunal can be attained and the faith of the nations in the fact of its attainment confirmed, disarmament will be nearer and the grievous burdens which the maintenance of armies imposes upon industry will be lifted. America will hail the glad day.

BIBLIOGRAPHICAL AIDS

The emphasis in this section, following the earlier volumes of the *Presidential Chronologies* series, is on the administration years but includes critical notations that may serve to a better understanding of the President both before and after the White House.

Additional titles can be found in the bibliographies compiled by Sievers (see Biographies below). Most students have access to *Reader's Guide to Periodical Literature*, *Social Science and Humanities Index*, and *Writings in American History*.

Chronological information for the period may be supplemented on two levels. Secondary school students can easily consult the *Encyclopedia of American History*, edited by Richard B. Morris, revised edition (New York, 1965). College history majors and graduate students will find both the content and the bibliography of the *Harvard Guide to American History* and the American Historical Association's *Guide to Historical Literature* indispensable aids.

Books currently available in paperback editions are noted with an asterisk after the title.

SOURCE MATERIALS

To date there is no printed edition of the Benjamin Harrison Papers. In 1964 the microfilm of the Harrison Papers became available, as did the *Index to the Benjamin Harrison Papers* (The Library of Congress, Presidents' Papers Index Series, 333 pages). This *Index*, available from the Government Printing Office, Washington, D.C., covers the 151 microfilm reels (representing all the Harrison holdings in L.C.) and identifies nearly 70,000 items dealing with Harrison's life and career. Readers and researchers are referred to the "Introduction" of the *Index*. It features a serviceable "Provenance" and offers practical guidelines for the use of the microfilm that is available on inter-library loan from the Library of Congress and other large city, state and university libraries. Also complete sets as well as individual reels are available for purchase by institutions and private citizens.

Only in 1945 were the Harrison papers declared "generally open for the use of students." The almost unbelievable story behind the papers and uncompleted attempts at Harrison's biography is briefly told in Sievers (see Biographies below), in *Benjamin Harrison: Hoosier Warrior*, in the Preface to the second edition (revised) that appeared in 1960.

The source materials below are only those which apply to Benjamin Harrison's role as candidate, President, and ex-President.

Hedges, Charles, compiler. *Speeches of Benjamin Harrison, Twenty-third President of the United States.* (New York, 1892). A complete collection of his public addresses from February 1888 to February 1892, chronologically classified; embracing all his campaign speeches, letter of acceptance, inaugural address, and numerous speeches delivered during several national tours. It also contains extracts from his messages to Congress. The compiler, Charles Hedges, a reporter for the Associated Press, often traveled with the Presidential party and regarded this book as "a series of instantaneous photographs" of a man in action and of a President who showed the rare artistic combination of speaking and writing well under varying conditions. Each extract is prefaced with the compiler's historical evaluation of the event.

Harrison, Benjamin. *Public Papers and Addresses of.* (Washington, D.C., 1893). This official volume is valuable and more comprehensive than the unofficial work of Hedges. In the first 160 pages are reproduced full texts of letters accepting the first and second nomination, the inaugural, and the four annual messages to Congress. In the second section, consisting of some 60 pages, are reproduced special messages to Congress. Harrison's veto messages, as well as Presidential proclamations and orders, complete the contents. Most major libraries have this compilation.

— — — —. *This Country of Ours.* (New York, 1897). The best way to describe this volume is to cite Harrison's own prefatory remarks. "This volume does not deal at all with the material resources of our country. It has nothing to do with lands, or merchandise or markets. It is not a philosophical dissertation on civics, nor a commentary on the Constitution. It is a modest attempt to give my readers a view of the machinery of our National Government in motion, and some instruction as to the relations and uses of its several parts. The larger part of the contents of the book appeared in the *Ladies' Home Journal* during the years 1896-97. That text has been carefully revised and much new matter added. The purpose of the book is to give a better knowledge of things that have been too near and familiar to be well known. We stumble over things that are near our toes. I hope it may also tend to promote an intelligent patriotism and a faithful discharge of the duties of citizenship." As noted, in the chronological section, the author's hopes were realized when this volume went through several editions and was translated into five foreign languages.

— — — —. *Views of An Ex-President,* comp. by Mary Lord Harrison. (Indianapolis, 1901). Published after Harrison's death by his second wife this volume had the merit of collecting the ex-President's addresses and writings on subjects of public interest between 1894 and 1901. Part I reproduced Harrison's six lectures on constitutional history and law (delivered at Stanford University in 1894—see Chronology), as well as the two papers that appeared in the *North American Review* under the title of "Musings on Current Topics." It is interesting to note that these papers represent Harrison's final public utterances on armed intervention, colonialism, and the obligations following the status of world power. Part II contains a collection of Harrison's formal and informal addresses and articles covering such broad topics as law reform, education, ecumenism and the "compulsory dishonesty" of free-silver leaders.

BIOGRAPHIES

Sievers, Harry J. *Benjamin Harrison: Hoosier Warrior.* Chicago, 1952; New York, 1960, second edition (revised). This opening volume of a trilogy, subtitled "Through the Civil War Years, 1833-1865," traces Harrison's boyhood on the family farm in North Bend, Ohio, through the early days of his marriage, political beginnings, and struggle to make a living as an Indiana lawyer. Boldness and courage in the Civil War won him the devotion of his soldiers and earned for him a brigadier general's star.

— — — —. *Benjamin Harrison: Hoosier Statesman.* New York, 1959. This middle volume recounts the Harrison story from the Civil War to the White House, 1865-1888. The man who returned to civilian life at 32 gained a national reputation as a courtroom lawyer who also rose quickly in Republican politics. He served as junior senator from Indiana during the Arthur and Cleveland Administrations. This book depicts the "middle years" of the little Hoosier who won the G.O.P. Presidential nomination in 1888 and scored an electoral victory over Grover Cleveland.

— — — —. *Benjamin Harrison: Hoosier President.* Indianapolis and New York, 1968. This final volume is the first definitive treatment of the administration (1889-1893) of the Nation's Centennial President. Though a rock-ribbed Republican, he emerged "His Own Boss" and defied the party by insisting on civil service reforms in the heyday of the Spoils System. He also attempted, without success, to bring the vote to Southern Negroes. Ranked by many historians as an average but obscure White House occupant, Harrison is portrayed as honest, capable and a constitutional President in an era of crooked politics.

Useful but not readily available is the *Benjamin Harrison Memorial Commission Report* (House Doc. No. 154, 77th Congress, 1st Session). Washington, D.C., 1941. Exhibit 2, pp 19-210 carries an interesting but somewhat inaccurate account of the Harrison family in American History. The author, who did not have access to the Harrison papers in the Library of Congress, was Ross F. Lockridge, Jr.

ESSAYS

The student interested in the Administration of Benjamin Harrison will be disappointed in most older encyclopedia accounts. New material is beginning to appear. Recommended are the accounts in the *World Book Encyclopedia*, published by Field Enterprises in Chicago, and the forthcoming sketch in the *Encyclopedia Americana*.

The essay by A.T. Volwiler in the *Dictionary of American Biography* is useful but dated. New interpretations are forthcoming and the student should periodically consult the usual indices for current treatments in scholarly journals. Also recommended is the annual list of Ph.D. dissertations in progress.

MONOGRAPHS AND RELATED AREAS

Baker, George W. "Benjamin Harrison and Hawaiian Annexation: A Reinterpretation," *Pacific Historical Review* (September, 1964).

Carpenter, Frank G. *Carp's Washington.* New York, 1960.

Dozer, D.M. "Benjamin Harrison and the Presidential Campaign of 1892," *The American Historical Review* (October, 1948).

Hays, Samuel P. *The Response to Industrialism, 1885-1914.* Chicago, 1957.*

Knoles, George H. *The Presidential Campaign and Election of 1892.* Palo Alto, 1942.*

La Feber, Walter. *The New Empire: An Interpretation of American Expansion.* Ithaca, 1963.

McMurry, Donald L. "The Bureau of Pensions During the Administration of President Harrison," *Mississippi Valley Historical Review* (now *Journal of American History*) Vol. 13 (1926).

Peck, Harry Thurston. *Twenty Years of the Republic, 1885-1905.* New York, 1907.

Pollard, James E. *The Presidents and the Press.* New York, 1947.

Volwiler, A.T. "Harrison, Blaine, and American Foreign Policy, 1889-1893," *Proceedings of American Philosophical Society,* LXXIX, No. 4 (November, 1938), 644.

————— (editor). *The Correspondence Between Benjamin Harrison and James G. Blaine, 1882-1893.* Philadelphia, 1940.

THE GILDED ERA

De Santis, V.P. *Republicans Face the Southern Question.* Baltimore, 1959.

Faulkner, H.U. *Politics, Reform, and Expansion.* New York, 1959,* concentrates on the decade 1890 to 1900.

Ginger, Ray. *The Age of Excess.* New York, 1965,* discusses U.S. History from 1877 to 1914 in a stimulating book.

Hirshson, S.P. *Farewell to the Bloody Shirt.* Bloomington, Ind., 1962.

Morgan, H.W. (editor). *The Gilded Age: A Reappraisal.* Syracuse, 1963,* contains useful essays on the rise of the city and the intellectual development of America.

White, L.D. *The Republican Era.* New York, 1958, is the best study of governmental machinery, 1869-1901. Useful for Harrison's reform in Cabinet matters.

While the above listed volumes are readily available, no serious student can fail to digest two superb analyses of the political system of the Gilded Age written by men who studied it first hand: James Bryce, *The American Commonwealth,* * 2 vols. New York, 1888, and Moisei Ostrogorski, *Democracy and the Organization of Political Parties.* * New York, 1902. Vol. 2 deals with the United States and Vol. 1 with England.

THE PRESIDENCY

Bailey, Thomas A. *Presidential Greatness: The Image and the Man from George Washington to the Present.* New York, 1966.* This well known author in the field of American history and biography lists more than forty yardsticks to measure presidential ability. Subjective and critical this text tests White House character by his standards. For the Harrison era it should be compared with Leonard D. White, *The Republican Era* (cited above) and his criteria. The treatment is topical, not chronological.

Binkley, Wilfred E. *The Man in the White House: His Powers and Duties.* Revised edition. New York, 1964.* A handy treatment that should be used along with

— — — —. *President and Congress.* 3rd revised edition. New York, 1967.*

Brown, Stuart Gerry. *The American Presidency: Leadership, Partisanship and Popularity.* New York, 1966.* The subtitle reveals an apparent tendency to equate all three presidential qualities.

Corwin, Edward S. *The President: Office and Powers.* 4th edition. New York, 1957.* Still a classic that defines the constitutional role of Presidents.

Heller, Francis H. *The Presidency: A Modern Perspective.* New York, 1960*.* In addition to five sprightly chapters dealing with "What We Expect," "What We Provide," "How and Whom We Select," "The Powers of the Office" and "The Measure of the Job," Professor Heller sets down a personal guide to readong on "The Presidency." This original study is a valuable contribution to the Random House Series in Political Science.

Kane, Joseph Nathan. *Facts About the Presidents.* New York, 1960.* A handy, comprehensive record of each President. It gives comparative and biographical data.

Koenig, Louis W. *The Chief Executive.* New York, 1964. This authoritative study of presidential power can be studied with the same author's paperback volume.

—— — —. *Official Makers of Public Policy: Congress and the President.* Glenview, Ill., 1967.*

Laski, Harold J. *The American Presidency.* New York, 1940.* A classic now available in paperback as a title in the Universal Library books published by Grossett and Dunlap, Inc., N.Y.

Neustadt, Richard E. *Presidential Power.* New York, 1964.* A provocative analysis of the function and authority of the Presidency by a professor of government who served on Truman's White House staff and acted as special consultant to John F. Kennedy during the transition of 1960-61. Although the author concentrates on the Presidency since F.D.R., he discusses "weak" and "strong" Presidents, by demonstrating the dynamic interrelation of power and politics.

Rossiter, Clinton. *The American Presidency.* 2nd edition. New York, 1960.* A useful study by a Cornell professor whose companion volume in paperback, *Parties and Politics in America* enjoys popularity.

Schlesinger, Arthur Meier. "Historians Rate United States Presidents," *Life,* XXV (November 1, 1948), 65 ff.

—— — —. "Our Presidents: A Rating by Seventy-five Historians," *New York Times Magazine.* July 29, 1962, 12 ff.

NAME INDEX

TITLES IN THE OCEANA
PRESIDENTIAL CHRONOLOGY SERIES

Reference books containing Chronology — Documents — Bibliographical Aids for each President covered.

Series Editor: Howard F. Bremer

1. GEORGE WASHINGTON *
   edited by Howard F. Bremer
2. JOHN ADAMS *
   edited by Howard F. Bremer
3. JAMES BUCHANAN *
   edited by Irving J. Sloan
4. GROVER CLEVELAND **
   edited by Robert I. Vexler
5. FRANKLIN PIERCE *
   edited by Irving J. Sloan
6. ULYSSES S. GRANT **
   edited by Philip R. Moran
7. MARTIN VAN BUREN **
   edited by Irving J. Sloan
8. THEODORE ROOSEVELT **
   edited by Gilbert Black
9. BENJAMIN HARRISON *
   edited by Harry J. Sievers
10. JAMES MONROE *
    edited by Ian Elliot
11. WOODROW WILSON **
    edited by Robert Vexler
12. RUTHERFORD B. HAYES *
    edited by Arthur Bishop
13. ANDREW JACKSON **
    edited by Ronald Shaw
(14, 15, 16 to be announced)
17. HARRY S TRUMAN ***
    edited by Howard Furer
18. JAMES MADISON *
    edited by Ian Elliot

  * 96 pages, $3.00/B, available now.
 ** 128 pages, $4.00/B, available now.
*** 160 pages, $5.00/B, available late 1969.

P A 3.
× ◡ ,   1 7 1. 2. 6 1